EXPERIENCE THE HEALING POWER OF THE EARTH

The room was so thick with sage smoke that I could barely see the healer although he sat only two feet away. His assistant set the pan containing the coals down on the Navajo rug spread on the floor between us and left. I watched carefully as the healer rummaged through an old, battered suitcase, from which he retrieved a huge, clear quartz crystal and an eagle feather. He sprinkled more sage on the coals, fanned them with the feather, and began to chant a prayer to the Great Spirit. As the coals glowed fiery red in the half-light and the room grew smokier still, he gazed at me through his crystal. He then proceeded to divine my situation with startling accuracy.

Native American medicine people and healers from other tribal and shamanic cultures all over the world use stones and crystals when doctoring patients. Because they are incarnate in everything around us, many cultures venerate stones as an indestructible and absolute reality, the source of all life, and the very bones of Mother Earth.

Crystal Medicine is a triumphant celebration of ancient and modern healing ways that incorporate all the many gifts of the Earth into a realistic new path to personal wholeness and well-being.

"Marguerite Elsbeth has a unique insight into the physical and spiritual properties of stones and crystals. *Crystal Medicine* is a must-have reference book for all crystal users and healers."

Catherine Bowman
author of *Crystal Awareness*
and *Crystal Ascension*

"*Crystal Medicine* has all the earmarks of becoming a best-seller in the field. It presents fresh information, in a well organized manner, and is superbly written."

Carol Dow
author of *Sarava: Afro-Brazilian Magick*

ABOUT THE AUTHOR

Marguerite Elsbeth (*Senihele*, Sparrow Hawk) is a professional diviner, and a student of Native American and European folk healing. Since 1984 she has published numerous articles in *Dell's HORO-SCOPE, The Mountain Astrologer, Llewellyn's Magical Almanac* and other publications, and is co-author of *The Grail Castle: Male Myths and Mysteries in the Celtic Tradition* and *The Silver Wheel: Women's Myths and Mysteries in the Celtic Tradition* with Kenneth Johnson. Marguerite is proud of her Lenni Lenape (Delaware) Native American ancestry, and is also a hereditary Sicilian strega. She currently resides on a Pueblo Indian reservation in the desert Southwest.

TO WRITE TO THE AUTHOR

If you wish to contact the author or would like more information about this book, please write to the author in care of Llewellyn Worldwide, and we will forward your request. Both the author and publisher appreciate hearing from you and learning of your enjoyment of this book and how it has helped you. Llewellyn Worldwide cannot guarantee that every letter written to the author can be answered, but all will be forwarded. Please write to:

Llewellyn Worldwide Ltd.
P.O. Box 64383, Dept. K258–5
St. Paul, MN 55164-0383, U.S.A.

Please enclose a self-addressed, stamped envelope for reply or $1.00 to cover costs. If outside the U.S.A., enclose international postal reply coupon.

CRYSTAL MEDICINE

MARGUERITE ELSBETH

2000
Llewellyn Publications
St. Paul, Minnesota 55164-0383, U.S.A.

FIRST EDITION
Third Printing, 2000

Cover design by Lisa Novak
Cover photo by Leo Tushaus
Editing and interior design by Connie Hill
Interior photos by Marguerite Elsbeth, Christine LeMay, John C.
    Werner, and Sandra Reading Kadisak
Color section photos © by Visuals Unlimited
Interior illustrations by Marguerite Elsbeth, Lisa Novak, and
    Tom Grewe
Diagrams on pp. 5, 33, 45, 55, and 57 by Giorgetta Bell McRee

Library of Congress Cataloging-in-Publication Data

Elsbeth, Marguerite, 1953–
    Crystal medicine / by Marguerite Elsbeth
        p. cm. --
    Includes bibliographical references and index.
    ISBN 1–56718–258–5 (trade paper)
    1. Crystals—Therapeutic use.   2. Precious stones—Therapeutic
use.   3. Minerals—Therapeutic use.   4. Crystals—Psychic aspects.
5. Precious stones—Psychic aspects.   I. Title.
RZ415.E39   1997
615.8'56—dc21   97-24492
                                                              CIP

Llewellyn Publications
A Division of Llewellyn Worldwide, Ltd.
St. Paul, Minnesota 55164-0383, U.S.A.
www.llewellyn.com

dedicate this book to the spirits that have gone before me, to my ancestors, to all my relatives, to the Elders and healers who have taught me what I know, that I may better serve the Great Spirit, and to all the people of Native America. It takes a lot of time, effort, and resources to perpetuate Native spiritual traditions. One excellent vehicle to support tradition is the building of *Oceti Wakan* (Sacred Fireplace), a healing center spiritually based in the Lakota (Sioux) tradition on the Pine Ridge Indian reservation. If you would like to help, please send donations to:

Zintkala Oyate
Peter V. Catches, President
Keeper of the Spotted Eagle Medicine
For Oceti Wakan (Sacred Fireplace)
P.O. Box 1936
Pine Ridge, SD 57770

OTHER BOOKS
BY MARGUERITE ELSBETH

The Grail Castle: Male Myths and Mysteries
in the Celtic Tradition (with Kenneth Johnson)

The Silver Wheel: Women's Myths and Mysteries
in the Celtic Tradition (with Kenneth Johnson)

CONTENTS

⇥ PART ONE ⇤

⇛ PART TWO ⇚

PHOTOGRAPHS AND ILLUSTRATIONS

COLOR SECTION

PREFACE

Mother Earth is the outer body of the Great Spirit. It is my belief that the true nature of the world will come into better focus when we realize our interconnectedness with Mother Earth and the creatures and things dwelling upon her turtle back. As the story goes in the Cherokee legend of Star Woman, the Earth herself comes from the sky. So the stars, planets, and constellations in relation to crystals and gemstones are included in this book, because indeed, we walk on stardust when we walk upon the pebbles, rocks, and minerals of the Earth.

My plan was to tell you about the latest, greatest, strangest crystal findings since 1986, a time when New Age "crystal crunching" was rapidly moving forward. It was late February, 1996, and I was headed to the Tucson Gem and Mineral Show in Arizona with my writing partner, Ken Johnson; however, the Great Mystery had other plans for me. Driving home in a blizzard the day before we were set to leave, I rolled my truck onto the median of the highway and was suddenly upside down facing north, when just a moment ago I had been right side up going south. I climbed out of the vehicle, virtually unscathed except for my pride.

This occurrence would have had a more significant bearing on this book had I been carrying a crystal or some other stone at the time, but I must admit that I was not. All I had with me were the rocks in my head, and I don't believe enough of them were significantly jarred loose to make a noticeable difference. I happen to like it here on present-day Earth, past life memories and close encounters of the fourth dimensional kind to the contrary. If there's residual "stuff" from my past that requires a psychic overhaul, or space aliens are disturbing my dreamtime, I've got to work with what I've got, right here, right now. There's no escape. It's all happening right here inside me.

I also have another reason for keeping my feet on good old terra firma. I don't want to disrespect the traditions of indigenous cultures who have always been here living in harmony with the Earth. To say that our knowledge of stones and how to use them comes from another planet or an ancient drowned civilization is to take away power from the natural peoples of Earth, who have worked with stones ever since time began. They know the stone spirits because they have always listened to the Earth Mother and her creatures. Indigenous peoples prophesied the current Earth changes long before modern society got on the bandwagon.

Technology teeters on the brink of cosmic rediscovery, and it is difficult to determine where prophecy and the current Earth changes might lead us as a collective world organism on or about the year 2000. It is important that we remain alert and aware as we evolve with depth and conscience toward the New Millennium, because ultimately the course of future world action is imprinted on the cosmic ethers by us. Rather than go to extremes, let us watch and listen to the Earth, so that we may act accordingly and without fear if and when the cataclysm comes, and meanwhile attend to the business of living in a way that meets the requisite and relentless needs of the human condition.

While I did not have the stone spirits in my truck on that fateful day I took it out for a roll in the snow (I do now), crystals and gemstones have played an integral role in bringing me to a viable point in the ongoing process of self-realization. The stone people—the

earth angels, devas, dwarves, elves and other elemental spirits resid-
ing in the mineral kingdom—have shared healing with me in
countless ways. They bring me the questions I need to ask of
myself, the answers that well up inside, and a sense of cosmic security in a rapidly changing world. This book is my way of acknowledging, blessing, and offering many thanks for their loving support.

—Marguerite Elsbeth
Cochiti, New Mexico
March 1997

NOTE FROM THE
PUBLISHER

Some remedies and processes discussed in this book involve toxic
or potentially dangerous materials. These have been indicated with
appropriate cautions and a skull and crossbones symbol. Anyone
interested in using the described materials or processes should be
aware that they are potentially dangerous to one's health. This is
not a medical book, and is not intended to encourage the use of
the alternative medical remedies and practices described herein.
The publisher takes no position on the effectiveness or accuracy of
the procedures, but is only reporting cultural or historical practices.

CRYSTAL CONSCIOUSNESS FOR THE NEW MILLENNIUM

LEAVING A RECORD

Several years before I took my reliable, turbo-charged Chevy S10 Blazer sledding on the icy highway, it broke down in Sedona, Arizona. According to Dick, the weathered, redneck mechanic who repaired the Chevy's drive housing and lubed its dried-out differentials, I had entered the "crystal crunching" capitol of the free world. Four days cruising the town on foot proved him right. Crystals, and the folks supposedly "crunching" them, were everywhere. Stone devotees pervaded the galleries, coffee houses, bookstores, and supermarkets. They sat on the red rocks in varying degrees of lotus posture, gazing at the sky with a crystal in the open palm of each hand.

Peking Man was the first Crystal Cruncher we know about. His crystal collection, found in a cave in China, dates all the way back to the Old Stone Age. Crystals, gemstones, and minerals have continued to hold humankind spellbound in one way or another.

Tribal cultures all over the world have always reverenced and worked with stones for communicating, healing, or seeing the future. Rock-writing was one of the earliest forms of communication.

Ancient Egyptians engraved their *Book of the Dead*[1] onto semi-precious stones that had been cut into symbolic forms.[2]

The Celts left their tracks literally etched in stone in the ancient Celtic alphabet called Ogham, and they built giant stone circles such as Stonehenge. The Mimbres, Anazasi, and other North American Indians cut inscriptions and pictures called petroglyphs into cliff faces and rocks. The Gypsies, whose origins may be traced back to India, are famous for scrying with crystal balls. Peruvian Indians believed emeralds to be the daughters of the goddess Umina, and bore them as gifts to her shrine in order that she might visit with her offspring.[3] Crazy Horse carried a pebble behind his ear, which made him bulletproof.[4] The current trend of wearing or carrying a leather- or metal-wrapped crystal for protection, energy, or power is an idea borrowed from the Cherokee Indian Nation.[5] The Lakota Sioux Indians perform the *yuwipi* ceremony using the power of sacred rocks.[6] Quartz crystal divination for second sight, called *makahyohoh* by some Southwest Pueblo Indians, is a method also used by Navajos, Creeks, Lakota, and a host of other tribes.

Scientists and physicists researched the properties of stones, while alchemists believed that eternal life was gleaned by turning lead into gold and true enlightenment found in the Stone of the Wise, that radiant jewel of illuminated mind.

Indigenous peoples and scientists have reached a point of mutual agreement that the magnetism produced by an electric current is inherent in the atomic structure of certain stones. Galena, a pure lead ore, is a prime example, long known for its use as the crystal in the radio. Likewise, magical thinkers and quantum physicists currently agree that electromagnetic energy is the physical source

---

1 E. A. W. Budge, *The Book of the Dead* (London: Longman & Co., 1895).

2 Kunz, George. *The Curious Lore of Precious Stones* (New York: Dover Publications, Inc., 1971), p. 225.

3 Ibid, p. 247–8.

4 Crow Dog, Leonard and Richard Erdoes. *Crow Dog: Four Generations of Sioux Medicine Men* (New York: HarperCollins Publishers, Inc., 1995), p. 116.

5 Hudson, Charles, *The Southeastern Indians* (Tennessee, The University of Tennessee Press, 1976), p. 168.

6 Crow Dog and Erdoes, *Crow Dog*, p. 115.

of ether (the fifth force or element, in addition to fire, water, air and earth) in which all creatures and things exist. This method, originating in a branch of physics that deals with the relationship between electricity and magnetism, draws a bridge across the ever-narrowing chasm between ordinary and non-ordinary reality as perceived by mystics and shamans.

Those of us who are out of touch with the land that we live on still have the love of precious gems imprinted in our hearts. I think we have continued our relationship with the mineral kingdom because stones, beyond their beauty and brilliant color, give us a sense of permanence in a rapidly changing world.

Crystals, gems, and minerals help us to comprehend the electromagnetic aspect of dense matter. Once we become aware of the basic composition of matter in its initial pattern of electromagnetic substance, we can recreate our environment according to the blueprint of Nature. In this way, we may bring an influx of harmony into the chaotic energies of the emerging New Millennium.

Sandra Reading Kadisak

Petroglyphs on Newspaper Rock
This prehistoric record is found in Canyonlands National Park, Utah.

SEED CRYSTALS

Now, perhaps more than at any time in history, we are aware that we stand on the back of a breathing, feeling, shifting, changing, living entity, and that this "body-earth" is also host to other innumerable, differentiated forms. In fact, she throbs like a heartbeat with the electromagnetic pulse of cosmic life.

The body-earth, this planetary body upon which we live, is seeded by the heat, warmth, and light of the sun, the heart center of our solar system. So, we may call the sun Sky Father because he is a primal consort of Mother Earth.[9] Because we are children of both the sun-star and the body-earth, our bodies represent the cosmos in miniature. Our bodies are the seed crystals of the sun, the moon, the planets, and the stars.

Everything happens within the body. If we want change, we have to go inside the body to make it happen. All meditation and psychic phenomena occur through the body. When we question ourselves, we must look within the body, to our mind and feelings and instincts, for an answer. And the answer comes through the crystalline bones of our ancestors, the kingdom of stone buried deep within the heart of body-earth.

The stone kingdom is currently assisting the Earth Mother in her struggle to gain our attention. Like photons and neutrinos, crystals and gemstones cut through the surface of earth to nourish our hearts and minds with seed-thoughts that awaken us to know and choose our own destiny.[10] Ostensibly, one might say that Mother Earth is seeding us with images that prompt us to make a concerted effort to focus on the ecology. These images may be essential to the extended life of our planet.

One such image is that of the wounded healer. Many of us feel like war casualties these days, so we are very much interested in acknowledging our pain and seeking a point of inner wholeness. I

---

9 While I prefer to use American Indian terms such as Sky Father and Mother Earth to depict the earth and the sun as personal, physical aspects of the Great Spirit, keep in mind that various tribal cultures have their own gender attributions for the heavenly bodies of our solar system.

10 Photons and neutrinos are some of the invisible elements released when a star explodes.

perceive this hands-on experience of physical, emotional, mental, and/or spiritual discomfort as a teacher. In this way we are taught to gather up and foster the sacred seeds of healing within ourselves. Remembering our innate wholeness allows the seed-crystal images we have gathered to grow in such a way as to bring true healing to ourselves and others, because we will no longer feel separated from the body of Mother Earth, and hence, from all of Nature. So, beyond the pleasurable, profitable, or magical uses they afford humankind, I believe that crystals, gemstones, and minerals are tools for guidance in helping us to understand our collective destiny as a whole earth organism, and that through stones we may heal and be healed of the woes that beset Nature at this tumultuous time in the history of our planet.

CHANGING EARTH

For reasons including greed, ignorance, fear, and force of habit, many people choose to ravish this living body-earth by misusing and abusing both natural and manmade materials, chemicals and energies. We add insult to injury with a total lack of respect and reverence for her body, and the creatures and things dwelling within her biosphere of influence. In turn, the Earth Mother attempts to defend herself by bringing about climatic and terrestrial changes that unsettle and threaten the survival of humankind.

Often I think we are misled by our notion that humankind is the most highly developed species on the planet. Intelligence cannot be measured by brains and opposable thumbs alone. We, in our collective ignorance, have long believed that we are here to assist Nature. We seem to think that without our help, the world will fail. We only have to look around to see that our high-tech meddling has wrought more harm than good in contributing to the current shift in planetary cycles we are now experiencing.

The potential for holes to develop in the ozone layer has increased because we can't live without cars and refrigerators. The South American rainforest, our main source of oxygen and home to literally thousands of undocumented medicinal plants, rare, exotic birds and animals, and aboriginal tribes (some of which have never known a hint of so-called civilization), is being ripped apart in order to produce more fast-food hamburgers. The Siberian wilderness is plundered in order to harvest its vast, rich timber and mineral resources, killing off the last of its shamans in the process. Nuclear waste is buried in the earth (particularly in the Southwest region of the United States, one of *our* last bastions of wilderness), considering but not heeding the devastating effect this will have on future generations. Weapons are created for war while people are hungry, sick, and homeless. Our waking hours are spent thinking of new and improved ways to annihilate the people, creatures, and things indigenous to the land, while the dichotomy of this seeming mass movement toward interglobal genocide is that all of our contrary actions are rooted in the collective fear of death!

Death is but another connecting link in the continuum of life. When we die, we are free to experience the whole of creation. Maybe this movement toward planetary annihilation is a backward way of remembering the oneness we share with all creatures and things.

Perhaps the more drastic results of our inconsiderate actions—the global warming, floods, earthquakes, and diseases that now threaten our survival—are the Earth Mother's attempts to rid her body of inharmonious, rapidly metastasizing human cells, or perhaps these earth changes are a result of natural cycles and have nothing to do with us at all.

Consider the asteroid named Eros which, even as I write these words, is hurtling through the cosmos toward the earth at breakneck speed. It is supposed to arrive between the years 1998 and 2012, and bring about the end of the world as we know it, in a time span that coincides with Hopi and Maya Indian prophecy. Isn't it ironic that unless the nuclear missiles the United States government plans to shoot into space mark their intended target and cause the asteroid to veer off course, in the end love (Eros) may kill us all? Should this happen, is it a blessing or a curse for our planet? Are we responsible for the final destruction, or, like the dinosaur, are we simply a part of Nature's changing way?

INTRODUCTION

I know a group of eco-conscious New Age spiritual seekers who are eagerly waiting for the world to blow up so that they can become galactic humans in the photon belt of life. In fact, as we near the year 2000, it seems that many of us are caught up in striving to reach the pinnacle of evolutionary development. What does this mean? How can we ultimately peak out if the spiral dance of life is unbroken? Eternity means that there is no beginning or end, so just because the world *as we know it* dies doesn't mean that there's nothing more to follow. It simply means that we are too attached to the present form of earth and it's inhabitants.

I have never understood the idea of perfect spiritual attainment. All this focus on becoming one of the chosen few galactic humans sounds arrogant and exclusivistic. It seems to me that perfection is always an accident, that we just "luck out" in our set of circumstances. We happen to "get it right" because there is synchronicity in the divine, universal scheme of things and we have entered the flux and flow.

Tribal peoples have never cared much for the idea of perfection, either. In fact, indigenous craftspeople will always create a tiny, deliberate mistake in their beadwork or weavings or whatever. A Lakota Indian woman says of the intentional flaws in her intricate beadwork designs, "That's the Indian way."

In search of spiritual *depth* as well as spiritual *growth*, we are prompted to look at the probable cause and effect of the New Millennium from another, more positive, and inclusive point of view. We can deepen our knowledge and understanding forever with all of time at our disposal. We don't have to struggle to gain the top of the mountain right here, right now. By joining the masses rather than standing alone looking down at them, we get to indulge in empathy, compassion, and shared endeavor, and maybe heal a few terrestrial wrongs in the process.

HEALING STONED

We have established that stones contain electromagnetic energy. This includes fire (electricity) from the sun, water (magnetism) from the moon, and various elemental energetics combining fire, water, air, and earth, as transmitted through the other planets and stars of our solar system. As mentioned earlier, the elements contained in the sun, moon, planets, and constellations are also integral components of the human body. Because stones resonate with the electromagnetic energies and star-body elements within our own bodies, we are attracted to them.

Like our modern-day quantum physicists, Pagan medicine men, wise women, and shamans have been looking up at the sky to determine the fate of humankind. When we look to the stars and planets for direction and guidance in our lives here on Earth, we call it astrology. Astrology was originally an offshoot of astronomy, the study of heavenly bodies. Because stones contain the

The Author at Stonehenge
These standing stones formed an astronomical observatory, circa 2000–1800 B.C.

same elemental composition of the stars and planets, we can use basic astrology as a guide in determining their attributes and characteristics and how we may work with them to benefit ourselves and others.

I have noticed in my work that people are usually attracted to stones that correspond with a deficient area of the body, mind, or heart, or they are drawn to stones that may enhance their current phase of evolutionary development. They may simply feel in harmony with the vibrations put out by a particular crystal, gem, or mineral. Whatever the attraction may be, my experience has been true that we are able to receive the psychic imprint of Nature through meditative or even proximal contact with stones, once we know where and how to look. Nature has given us an example of cosmic perfection in the internal structure of stones, because the inner molecular matrix of crystals, gems, and minerals is always synchronistically and mathematically correct, a scientific idea that we will also explore in more detail.

Finally, stones reflect back at us the internal workings of Nature, sharing with us the secrets of creation and answering our questions about life in the process. We may experience the cosmic synchronicity set forth in Nature when we learn to listen to the spirits that live in and talk through stones, even as our Pagan ancestors did and as contemporary Pagan people continue to do. Then it will become apparent that stones are actually mirrors for our sentient awareness, for when we can instinctively feel the vibrations stones are putting out, we can attune ourselves accordingly. Spiritual and magical practitioners from all over the world give credence to this fact, and in this book I will share specific scientific, alchemical, shamanic, and magical techniques that will deepen the possibility for personal communication with the mineral kingdom.

Perhaps we may change the seeming tailspin course of history as we enter into the New Millennium, perceive the infinite Great Spirit in Mother Earth, or even stumble upon the Stone of the Wise, as we drop our consciousness down into the heart of matter and begin to earth it with stone.

PART ONE

PART ONE

1

SOUND AND LIGHT

FIRST THE STONE

The rock is the oldest god, according to Leonard Crow Dog, a Lakota Sioux medicine man. The Lakota address the Great Spirit as *Tunkashila*, Grandfather. *Tunka* means rock. They say that the rock was here before everything else, that everything will perish someday but the rock will never die.[1]

Like many other indigenous peoples, the Lakota know that rocks are sacred because spirits dwell in them. Talking stones—tiny crystals and agates gathered from ant hills—fill their gourd rattles. Just as the Celts once worshiped in rings of giant standing stones, the Lakota pray over large rocks—such as the Medicine Rocks in Montana where Sitting Bull held a sundance one week before Custer's last stand.[2]

Because the Lakota also believe that we can heal or divine the future through dreams coming from rocks, there is the *yuwipi* ceremony, which uses the power inherent in the sacred stones. The *yuwipi* man is a stone dreamer, helping people solve their problems because the spirits in the stones talk to him and through him. In

---

1 Crow Dog and Erdoes, *Crow Dog*, pp. 115–116.
2 Ibid, pp. 116, 117.

3

order to hear the spirits in the stones, his hands and fingers are interlaced behind his back with rawhide strips, and he is completely covered with a star blanket. He is mummy-wrapped, both to aid his concentration and to unite him with *Tunkashila*. Then he is laid face down on a sage-covered floor, so the spirits can come and use him. The entire room is plunged into darkness, yet minute flashes of lightning can be seen sparking in the air. The Lakota call this *Tunka wasichun*, rock-power, and say that this phenomenon occurs because lightning and stones are related, such as when two flint stones are knocked together, creating sparks. When the ceremony ends, the *yuwipi* man doctors the sick and interprets what the rock spirits have told him.[3]

The *yuwipi* ceremony is very old and still in practice today. It reminds us that native peoples knew long ago that stones are a living combination of electromagnetism, the energies of fire and water, or the sun and moon. The mystery is *how* they knew prior to modern technology that stones could be accessed to help us heal and remember our innate wholeness.

PYTHAGOREAN THEORY

The ancient Greek philosopher Pythagoras, well known for his geometric interpretation of the universe, shared similar ideas regarding stones. Pythagoras studied in Egypt and Babylon, and possibly also among the Hindus and Druids. From his center in southern Italy, he taught occult mathematics, vegetarianism, and reincarnation to his few but fervent followers.

The Pythagorean Triangle is a design depicting evolutionary development. It includes the three alchemical principles known as Mercury ☿, Sulphur 🜍, and Salt ⊖, as well as the four elements: Fire △, Water ▽, Air △, and Earth ▽. Regarding the evolutionary process, Pythagoras intimates:

> First the stone, then the plant, then the animal, then the man; after man—the Great Spirit.

---

3 Ibid, pp. 117–124.

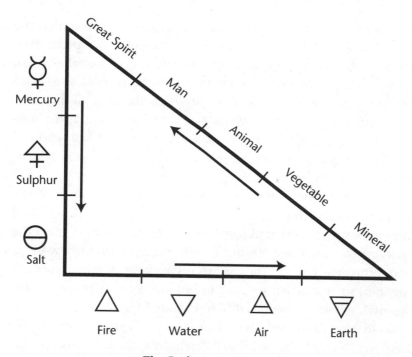

The Pythagorean Triangle

This chart illustrates Pythagoras' theory of evolutionary development, beginning with the stones of the Earth, and passing through stages toward godhood.

Notice that in this statement, stones come first and the God or Great Spirit comes last. This is not to imply that there is a cosmic hierarchy placing the God at the top and stones at the bottom of things; rather, it reminds us that all creatures and things—the plant, the animal, the man—are safe and secure between the stone, which is the visible foundation, and the God, the invisible source of life. This same concept is reflected in the Lakota word for the God: *Tunkashila*, Rock Grandfather.

In addition, I believe Pythagoras referred to the evolution of consciousness as well as physical evolution when he made this analogy, for while in some species one method of neurological relating is more highly developed that the others, every living being has one or a combination of sensory faculties, and can see, hear, smell, taste, or touch according to its individual ability to receive and transmit spirit energy. For example, while human beings have an opposable thumb, coupled with extreme intellectual capacities, the animal kingdom has a greater wealth of supersensory perception because of its reliance on instincts and feelings. Likewise, trees, plants, and herbs, and crystals, gems, and minerals emanate subtle vibrations that are detectable to sensitive, earth-centered humans.

The mineral kingdom shows us the manner in which the universe comes into being, and how spirit is born into the world of form. Every stone formation represents an aspect of the Great Spirit cloaked in dense matter.

Stones share the same electromagnetic patterning and atomic structure as the Earth-body, the human body, and all creatures and things in between. Different forms occur so that we may grasp the totality of the universe with our minds, which ordinarily work in linear terms. We separate the various life functions into classes and categories, such as when we refer to our concerns as being spiritual, mental, emotional, or physical in nature. In order to understand the world around us, we extend this linear way of thinking to the other kingdoms of Nature as well, including the spirit world, the animal, plant, and mineral kingdoms, and the elemental world. However, spirit remains the constant, living core of energy inhabiting all creatures and things, no matter how we seek to break down the equation.

STONED VIBRATIONS

Although stones appear to be standing still, they are moving to the vibratory energies of the universe, and are capable of transmitting and receiving the various rates of vibration that continuously flow in and out on the cosmic tides and the Earth-body, as well as through the body-earth. This is why stones are able to attract our attention, penetrate our senses, and assist in the healing process. Healing occurs because stones bring the hidden core of spirit energy to mind. Otherwise we might not remember our wholeness, our true and essential nature.

Nature is vibration. Vibration is sound. Ancient philosophers observed, "Out of sound, every form comes." Our life-cycles reflect matter as it is created through unending sound. Thoughts, dreams, images, visions, and actions all come to rest upon the reverberating waters of the cosmos, and these cosmic waves conduct the rhythm of life itself. This cosmic rhythm is inherent in the mineral kingdom.

Perhaps that is why Paracelsus, the well-known alchemist of the sixteenth century, said: "The element of water is the mother, seed, and root of all minerals."

Paracelsus knew that the primordial rock came rising out of the cosmic waters like the back of a giant turtle. While Paracelsus wasn't actually referring to the physical substance of water as we know it, it remains true that in order for a thing to become solid it must first be liquid in form. Hence the cosmic waters flow around us like the infinite yolk of an unborn egg, forming a limitless boundary and securing the sacred fire of the heart to the dense matter of the Earth-body and the body-earth (illustrated on page 11).

While our ordinary perceptions sometimes lack clarity due to the external limitations superimposed on our senses, we may learn to be alert to the ebb and flow of the cosmic currents and tides that move in and through our bodies. In fact, a person who remains conscious of the body can perceive varying rates of vibration through the non-ordinary senses, as shamans and mystics do. When we are awake to the body in a particular way, we may undergo a series of physiological and psychological changes at the cellular level, thus altering the vibrations we emit, and, consequently, the vibrations we absorb.

SPIRIT ENERGY

The breakdown of spirit energy into many subtle vibrations has been classified in various ways by different individuals.

Shamans see energy as spirits, gods, angels, and devas. The spirit energies embodied in the shamanic world view live on the World Tree. The World Tree grows in the center of the universe. It is an ancient mythological symbol for all of creation and our relationship to it, and stands as an Otherworldly roadmap, which may be used to observe and measure our existence. It is a guide that shamans use to navigate through the crossroads of life, and shamans of many cultures travel the axis of the World Tree to the three worlds:

- The upper world of Spirit

- The middle world in which we live

- The lower world of Soul

In some cultures, the World Tree is represented by a mound of earth, or formed by lumps of clay, or is shaped into a cylindrical stone.[4]

Opposites and Correspondences

Oriental philosophers associate spirit energy with the positive and negative distribution of forces, yang and yin. They believe that opposites brought together engender a mystic center through which spirit energy may flow in ceaseless perpetual motion.

"As above, so below" is the theory behind the alchemical world view. Alchemy recognizes the primal source of spirit energy as coming through human personality via the operations of the Sun and Moon, corresponding to gold and silver as well as to yang and yin, the intellect and the psyche, respectively.

Metaphysically speaking, the Sun corresponds to the macrocosm or the universe at large, while the Moon corresponds to the microcosm or the human being as a "universe in miniature." This relationship between the Sun and Moon is symbolic of the *whole* person, one who is balanced together with the constellations, the planets, and the elements.

The dualistic manifestation of spirit energy may be summarized as follows:

- Sun = Spirit = Above = Macrocosm = Mind = Electricity = Yang = Positive = Masculine = Active = Gold = Fire

---

4 Eliade, Mircea, *Shamanism: Archaic Techniques of Ecstacy* (Princeton: Princeton University Press, 1972), p. 426.

- Moon = Soul = Below = Microcosm = Psyche = Magnetism = Yin = Negative = Feminine = Passive = Silver = Water

All energy can be reduced to the four elements—Fire, Water, Air, and Earth. Fire and Air are active or yang, and Water and Earth are passive or yin. Esoteric thinkers also work with the energy of spirit in the form of ether, the fifth element, but physicists and scientists theorize about the existence of ether as a fifth element, and continue to classify all known substances into four categories of "known" energy:

- Electromagnetic energy, responsible for atomic structure and the emission of light.

- Gravity, considered to be the weakest known force, separate from all other known elements.

- Strong force, which binds the nucleus of atoms together.

- Weak force, responsible for certain kinds of radioactivity.

Conscience

If the whole is equal to the sum of its parts, it is easy to imagine that we may gain knowledge of the whole by coming to know and understand the parts. There is wisdom in this approach; however, as long as we persist in looking to the outer circumference of our experiences in order to substantiate our existence, we might never come to know the spirit within ourselves and all creatures and things.

"Look within" has unfortunately become a buzz phrase that has us all taking personal responsibility for the trials and tribulations of the critical problems that exist in the world today. On the one hand, this is not such a bad thing; better to have a conscience than to lack one. However, all too often our interior search for the guilty party results in self-doubt and shame over situations and conditions over which our control is slim or none. Therefore, we are not empowered by our findings.

I believe this occurs because we attempt to work on our problems alone, an unfortunate by-product of the dominant social tenet demanding that we be rugged individualists. Remember, everything happens in the body, so we must look within if we are ever to recollect our wholeness or assist in healing the Earth. Let us do so accompanied by the spirits, angels, devas, and gods of Nature, who are always willing to offer up guidance, protection, and information in exchange for acknowledgment, respect, and gratitude.

The spirits do not always speak in words, but we may hear them if we listen with the senses most attuned to picking up their subtle vibrations. Whether we receive our answers through telepathy, clairvoyance, clairaudience, telekinesis, or clairsentience doesn't matter, nor does it make any difference if our impressions come through the heart center or the big toe. What matters is our conscious receptivity to the physical manifestation of spirit energy in all its forms.

FIRE FROM THE SKY

As we have established, vibrations may be perceived through virtually any part of the body. However, the body's "headquarters" for non-ordinary vibratory perception are actually centers located in the central nervous system and the endocrine system running along the spinal cord. These centers, more commonly known as the chakras, form spirit energy vortices around these areas; their physical manifestation is composed of various ganglia, plexi, and glands. We will explore these centers in depth in chapter 4.[5]

Fire (electricity) dwells at the heart of the spirit energy centers. This fire is the living power at work in our bodies and animates us in every way. Like the cosmic waters surrounding the Earth, the centers serve as reservoirs from which we may draw spiritual, mental, emotional, and physical nourishment.

Just as our physical bodies are sensitive to heat and light, the food we eat, the air we breathe, and the ecosystem around us, so are our dreams, thoughts, words, and deeds influenced by the spirit energy centers. When the centers are flowing in harmony with Nature, we transmit and attract good vibrations, and so experience a sense of balance that includes robust good health, emotional, mental, and

---

5 I use the term "Spirit Energy Centers" instead of chakras to indicate that they are independent living centers.

spiritual well-being, and concordance with the world at large. When our centers are out of alignment, we experience the opposite effect—the proverbial "bad-hair day" (or life, as the case may be).

The spirit energy centers vibrate to the energies put forth by the planets and stars in the heavens as well as to the energies in the Earth. The planets provide the fire or electricity that motivates us to action, while the Earth gives us the water or magnetism that enables us to attract the fire from the sky. This is because the Earth is mostly water, although it also has a molten core. The stars further color the vibrations emanating through the planets.

Cosmic Water around the Earth's Molten Core
Cosmic water encompasses turtle island—the earth. This concept is a common tradition of many cultures, from Egyptian to Greek to Native American (see p. 7).

CHAPTER 1

Life's reactions to the vibrations emanating from the planets and stars is what astrology is all about. Astrology interprets Nature, and allows us to realize our natural purpose on Earth in accordance with the synchronicity of the cosmos. Therefore, if we observe and cooperate with Nature, we can produce certain results from the cosmic vibrations set in motion through us. We can change and improve our response to Nature and to life by improving our thinking, our habits, and our actions. If we wish to make the world a better place in which to live, we must start by refining our responses to instincts and feelings coming from within the body, which have their root in the influence of celestial vibrations.[6]

Stones, the bones of the Earth, are equally sensitive to the vibratory frequencies emitted from the planets and stars, and receive their various qualities, in part, from the heavenly bodies, just as we do.[7] The list of attributes and associations that follows will help you become more familiar with the planets and constellations (fixed stars) which—because everything in the universe is related to everything else through magical correspondence—constitute the signs of the zodiac, as well as the primary crystals, gems, and minerals embodying their vibrations.

---

6 George, Llewellyn, *A to Z Horoscope Maker and Delineator* (St. Paul, MN: Llewellyn Publications, 1969), pp. 21, 22.

7 We will investigate the scientific basis for this idea in chapter 4.

THE PLANETS

The Sun = Gold Ore

Element: Fire

Body-Earth: The back, spinal column, the thymus gland

Vibration: Loving

Keywords: Vitality, strength, creativity, regeneration, pride, ego

Qualities: Masculine, dynamic, electric

The Moon = Silver Ore

Element: Water

Body-Earth: The female reproductive system and its functions, the breasts, the esophagus, stomach, liver, gallbladder, bile ducts, pancreas, intestines

Vibration: Remembering

Keywords: Emotion, response, sympathy, moodiness, changeability

Qualities: Feminine, passive, magnetic

Mercury = Mercury Ore

Element: Air

Body-Earth: The brain, the lungs, the nervous system

Vibration: Neutralizing

Keywords: Communication, perception, versatility, intelligence

Qualities: Adaptable, transparent

Venus = Copper Ore

Element: Earth and Air

Body-Earth: The kidneys and lumbar region, the parathyroids

Vibration: Creating

Keywords: Fertility, affection, beauty, harmony

Qualities: Feminine-masculine, passive-dynamic, magnetic-electric

Mars = Iron Ore

Element: Fire

Body-Earth: The muscles and urogenital system, the gonads, the ovaries and testes

Vibration: Energizing

Keywords: Enthusiasm, initiative, courage, passion

Qualities: Masculine-feminine, dynamic-passive, electric-magnetic

Jupiter = Tin Ore

Element: Fire and Water

Body-Earth: The liver, the pituitary gland

Vibration: Expanding

Keywords: Kindness, generosity, prosperity, honesty, compassion, excess

Qualities: Masculine-feminine, dynamic-passive, electric-magnetic

Saturn = Lead Ore

Element: Earth and Air

Body-Earth: Gallbladder, spleen, skin, teeth, bones

Vibration: Concentrating

Keywords: Limitation, focus, practicality, security, stability, discipline

Qualities: Feminine-masculine, passive-dynamic, magnetic-electric

Uranus = Uranium Ore

Element: Ether, Air, Earth

Body-Earth: The circulatory system, the central nervous system

Vibration: Electrifying

Keywords: Liberation, eccentricity, originality, rebellion

Qualities: Masculine-feminine, dynamic-passive, electric-magnetic

Neptune = Platinum
Element: Water, Fire
Body-Earth: The thalamus, the sensory organs
Vibration: Dreaming
Keywords: Spirituality, idealism, dreams, illusion, confusion
Qualities: Feminine-masculine, passive-dynamic, magnetic-electric

Pluto = Sulphur
Element: Fire and Water
Body-Earth: The gonads, the cells, the reproductive function
Vibration: Transforming
Keywords: Power, regeneration, elimination, destruction
Qualities: Feminine-masculine, passive-dynamic, magnetic-electric

THE CONSTELLATIONS

Aries = Meta-Ankoleite
Element: Fire
Body-Earth: The head (see Mars)
Vibration: Initiating
Keywords: Action, assertion, naivete
Qualities: Masculine, dynamic, electric

Taurus = Thernadite
Element: Earth
Body-Earth: see Venus and Neptune
Vibration: Enduring
Keywords: Persistence, patience, intuition, stubbornness
Qualities: Feminine, passive, magnetic

Gemini = Sylvine

Element: Air

Body-Earth: Chest, arms, hands (see Mercury and Uranus)

Vibration: Communicating

Keywords: Dexterity, curiosity, flexibility

Qualities: Neutral, transparent

Cancer = Fluorite

Element: Water

Body-Earth: see the Moon

Vibration: Feeling

Keywords: Protection, emotion, sentimentality

Qualities: Feminine, passive, magnetic

Leo = Newberyite

Element: Fire

Body-Earth: see the Sun

Vibration: Revitalizing

Keywords: Drama, pride, creation, regality

Qualities: Masculine, dynamic, electric

Virgo = Jarosite, Aphtitalite

Element: Earth

Body-Earth: see Mercury

Vibration: Discriminating

Keywords: Diligence, sincerity, compassion, modesty

Qualities: Feminine, passive, magnetic

Libra = Stercorite

Element: Air

Body-Earth: see Venus

Vibration: Balancing

Keywords: Refinement, harmony, cooperation, indecision

Qualities: Masculine, dynamic, electric

Scorpio = Anhydrite

Element: Water

Body-Earth: see Mars and Pluto

Vibration: Immortalizing

Keywords: Determination, imagination, introspection, secret

Qualities: Feminine, passive, magnetic

Sagittarius = Quartz Crystal, Cat's Eye, Tiger's Eye, Aventurine

Element: Fire

Body-Earth: The thighs, also see Jupiter

Vibration: Enlivening

Keywords: Honesty, versatility, independence, prophecy

Qualities: Masculine, dynamic, electric

Capricorn = Autunite, Apatite, Collophanite

Element: Earth

Body-Earth: See Saturn

Vibration: Evaluating

Keywords: Reliability, prudence, caution, reservation

Qualities: Feminine, passive, magnetic

Aquarius = Halite

Element: Air

Body-Earth: The ankles (see Mercury and Uranus)

Vibration: Inspiring

Keywords: Humanitarianism, fellowship, invention

Qualities: Masculine, dynamic, electric

Pisces = Vivianite

Element: Water

Body-Earth: The feet (see Venus and Neptune)

Vibration: Imagining

Keywords: Kindness, humility, empathy, acceptance

Qualities: Feminine, passive, magnetic

⇥ CRYSTAL MEDICINE 1 ⇤
DRAWING ENERGY FROM THE EARTH

This first exercise is meant to familiarize you with the Earth-body and the body-earth—your physical body. Performing it regularly will help you to realize that the Earth is alive and very responsive to your attentions.

1. Find a comfortable spot where you can lie down. This spot can be anywhere—on the front lawn, the bed, or living room couch.

2.. Close your eyes. Relax. Breathe deeply into your belly and exhale fully several times.

3. Become aware of your physical body. Really get into it from your head down to your toes. Now, shift your attention to the Earth directly below you. Let feelings of gratitude and respect for the Earth spirits well up; stretch these sensations down through all the layers of the Earth until you become aware of the Earth's inner molten core.

4. Once you have reached the inner core of the Earth, feel all your fear, anxiety, and negativity drain down into the earth through your spinal column, beginning at the top and ending at the base of the spine. With your attention still focused at the base of the spine, begin to draw the pure, vital energy up from the Earth's core. Feel it slowly rise up through the spine until it reaches the top.

5. Open your eyes.

Crystals Make a Garden Grow
Earth's energy is transformed into the beauty of a garden, located at
the home of Sherry Black and Everett Buss in Crestone, Colorado.

2

CRYSTAL ALCHEMY

STAR WOMAN

The legend of Star Woman is a creation myth common to various Native American tribes. The Tsalagi or Cherokee people tell this version of the story:

One day, the most beautiful and beloved daughter of Asga Ya Galunlati, the father of all, was walking in her father's favorite garden when she heard the sound of drumming coming from under a little tree. Curious, she started digging beneath its roots until she created a hole and fell into it. Round and round she spun through the sky, falling from heaven to earth. It was a long way down.

The creatures that lived on the Earth at that time were very sensitive beings, but they lacked the spark of fire that enabled them to reason. Having no logic, only feelings, these creatures simply floated around on the waters that covered the world. When Asga Ya Galunlati saw his daughter spiraling through the sky, he called upon the winds and the creatures of Earth to help her land safely. At once, the impressionable creatures of the Earth looked up and saw something bright falling toward them. It was the maiden, shining like a star. The creatures sensed she was a gift from the heavens and knew instinctively that they must do something to protect her.

CHAPTER 2

They did not know that she carried clear quartz, ruby, topaz, jasper, emerald, rubellite, amethyst, pearl, fire opal, tourmaline, azurite, and aconite within her womb, crystals that symbolized the potential qualities of humankind.

Turtle was the first to react, offering his back to cushion the Star Maiden's fall. Many of the other creatures dove deep into the great ocean to gather soft, wet sand to support her fall against Turtle's hard shell. Both Water Spider and Muskrat claimed the honor of bringing up the protective firmament from the bottom of the sea, but whichever of the two put it there, the offshore loam was placed on Turtle's back, where it grew and grew, even as the Star Maiden continued to spiral down and down slowly through the sky, wafted by gentle winds. With the help of Buzzard, the dark, rich earth grew into rolling hills, snow-capped mountains, and verdant green valleys.

At last Star Woman landed on the solid earth that rose up from the sea, which some Indian people now call Turtle Island. The soil was fertile, and Star Woman's ample breasts gave forth squash and beans and corn. Her tears forged mighty rivers and placid, blue-mirrored lakes filled with fresh water.

Some Cherokees believe that all humans may trace their ancestry back to Star Woman, and that because she is the mother of all, we are all related. Indeed all people have received her blessing — the spirit of the sacred fire that ignites the mind to wonder, and inspires humankind to see the magical relationship between all creatures and things.[1]

The Falling Star

Star Woman is the story of a falling star. When the star fell into the cosmic waters, it seeded the cosmos with the potency for evolutionary development, because it contained the mineral elements necessary to create life on Earth (the clear quartz, ruby, topaz, jasper, emerald, rubellite, amethyst, pearl, fire opal, tourmaline, azurite, and aconite that Star Woman carried in her womb). The

---

1 Ywahoo, Dhyani, *Voices of Our Ancestors: Cherokee Teachings from the Wisdom Fire* (Boston: Shambhala Publications, 1987), pp. 29, 30, 31.

Star Woman myth provides us with the analogy of the creation of the Earth as a result of fire falling from the sky.

WE ALL COME FROM THE STARS

All matter in the universe is composed of atoms and possesses gravity, which comes from the magnetism of the Earth. This means that all creatures and things produce a magnetic force that causes other creatures and things to move toward them. The strength of this magnetic force depends on the size of the creature or thing, as well as the number and size of the atoms of which it is made. The greater the mass, the greater its gravitational and magnetic attraction. It is because of mass and gravity, and the effect of gravity on atoms, that we have the stars in the sky and life here on Earth.

Mass, gravity, and the effect of gravitational attraction on atoms enable human beings to exist in physical form. As a result of gravity and magnetic force on atoms, contraction and expansion between atoms is an ongoing process. The preservation of physical form is maintained by the conscious intake and expulsion of the air we breathe and the food we eat, both providing fuel that is then carried by the bloodstream to the various organs of the body. When the organs have received and absorbed the necessary nutritional requirements through the processes of assimilation, degenerate matter is released from the body and transformed back into Earth.

Matter used in this way gives us energy and animates our bodies to action. We usually think of this energy as being personal in nature, but we don't really own it. The energy that animates our bodies, that gives us volition, motivation, and will, is derived from external resources, such as food, light, water, and air—all physical aspects of the Great Spirit.

The energy in our bodies is the same as the thermonuclear energy in a supernova.[2] A supernova is a star that suddenly increases in brilliance, then gradually grows fainter in light; the Sun is such a

---

2 Thermonuclear energy refers to the heat energy released in nuclear fission, which causes atoms to break apart.

star. The qualities that cause this phenomenon to occur—contraction, expansion, and preservation—may be ascribed to the star-body as well as to the human body.

- Contraction is inertia or energy drawn inward.

- Expansion is momentum or an outward flow of motion.

Preservation maintains balance when meeting with the pull of gravity, and exists at the heart of all life-forms terrestrial or extraterrestrial.

So, like human development, stellar evolution follows a basic theme, consisting of two principle forces that polarize each other in order to maintain balance and harmony within the star body:

- The equilibration of gravity or contraction, which gathers matter through magnetic attraction.

- The expansion of atoms occurring in thermonuclear energy.

Stars are very hot. For example, our own daystar, the sun, is 93,000,000 miles away from the Earth's surface and we can still feel the heat. The sun was originally formed from a large cloud of hydrogen gas. Fusion caused the gas to explode outward while the hydrogen cloud collapsed inward under the force of its own gravity. Gravity and magnetism, collecting between the atoms, stopped the cloud from exploding altogether, so the hydrogen cloud became the sun-star. From an Earth-centered point of view, the moon is just as important as the sun. However, the moon no longer puts out its own light, but reflects the sun's light.

The energy created during the life-process of a supernova is also responsible for many of the known elements in the universe. When a supernova explodes, the blast forces these elements into space, producing great clouds of gas and dust. Shockwaves emerging through the coalescing gas and dust create new stars and planets. Consequently, the planets, and all life evolving on them, embody the elements of the stars.

The nuclear fission reaction in the core of an exploding star produces two kinds of particles: photons and neutrinos. Photons are light or x-rays, also known as cosmic rays. Neutrinos have no mass and are electrically neutral. When a star explodes, the photons are absorbed into the Earth, whereas the neutrinos pass right through it. Thus the Earth is seeded with star-body elements containing the matrices for mineral, vegetable, animal, and human life. These elements are very specific, and born in the mineral kingdom.

Sky Fire

Meteors and other heavenly bodies fall from the sky in a shower of crystal stardust. Once beneath the Earth's surface, they change into higher mineral forms composed of fire, water, air, and earth, the outer manifestations of ether or sky-fire.

The elements coalesce around the sky-fire at the center to create form. The earth-forms we are able to see are actually sky-clad fire centers. Every form is a center—so in essence, the center is everywhere. Everywhere we look, we can see sky fire in earth-form.

What is it that binds all earth-forms together, that connects all points in space, including the sun, the moon, the planets, and the stars? Strangely enough, the answer is something we use every day. The superglue that holds earth-forms in place, that causes vibratory motion to appear static to the naked eye, is consciousness. The fire of the mind grants us the ability to perceive the totality of thoughts, feelings, and impressions.

Consciousness acts as a mediator between spirit and matter. It intercepts images from the airwaves and feeds them to the psyche or soul. Because the images that flow down from the ethers into consciousness are then passed along by us to the other kingdoms of Nature and back into Earth, we co-create with the Great Spirit. The visions produced by mental fire become earth-forms because thoughts, feelings, and impressions are actually living things.

Human consciousness assists the cosmos in creating earth-forms. Whether or not we make an effort to participate as cosmic production managers, we are involved in the process anyway, as we are constantly creating via our habitual thought patterns and emotions. In fact, the minute an idea or image is emotionally charged, we make lightning. We give the sky-fire life and the power to come down into physical manifestation.

The thoughts and images that dominate the mind and emotions eventually become the outer circumstances of our life experience, because the mind is the thunderbolt and our emotions the water that tempers the metal of human personality. This process of personal transmutation is what alchemy is all about, and demands the hissing, steam-heat of fire on water, and the clanging and banging of metal on red-hot metal. Through tempering, our personalities are deepened, softened, and transformed.

Although mass attention is once again focused on crystals, gems, and minerals, it seems to me that we may be missing the alchemical point. Like children, we play with the shiny baubles of solidified sky-fire, but we don't take the stones seriously. Our instincts tell us that the pretty rocks mean something important, but we're not really sure what to do with them. We toy with various tantalizing notions; for instance, maybe we're from the Pleiades, so we'll sport crystals around our necks and live on blue-green algae because we are "not of this Earth."

Space Aliens and UFOs?

Reports of unidentified flying objects are scattered throughout history, from people in all walks of life. Sometimes sightings move beyond the classic fire-in-the-sky variety to include humanoid figures emerging from Earth-based, saucer-like or cylindrical crafts. More recently, we hear about the physio-psychological ramifications of abduction by space aliens. There are currently many books on the subject, such as John Grant Fuller's *The Interrupted Journey*,[3] which tells of the abduction of Betty and Barney Hill, or *Communion* by Whitley Streiber,[4] in which he describes alien interference with his entire family, replete with omens and extreme visceral responses.[3] A television broadcast recently showed an alien autopsy, replete with alien bodies allegedly taken from a spacecraft that crashed in Roswell, New Mexico, back in 1947; it looked real to me. There are many more examples too numerous to mention here. Our questions do not pertain to whether or not some of us are actually space aliens

---

3   Fuller, John Grant, *The Interrupted Journey* (Alexandria, VA: Time Life, Inc., 1993).
4   Streiber, Whitley, *Communion* (New York: Beech Tree Books, 1987).

or if UFOs exist, but address greater issues, such as: What are UFOs when viewed from a spiritual perspective? How can we apply our knowledge of the existence of UFOs to heal the human condition?

Carl Jung has explained our interest in UFOs as a projection of the desire for wholeness, an attempt by mass consciousness to heal polarized division in this revelatory age prior to the New Millennium.[5] Perhaps we are seeking wholeness because we feel separated from the Great Spirit, the Earth, the future, the past, our ancestors, the land, humanity, and ourselves. We have learned to believe that order and chaos, good and evil, shadow and light are distinct energies, when each is really an aspect of the whole. When we strive to achieve enlightenment only, and ignore the chaos inherent in human nature, we actually foster its growth!

The circle (i.e., flying saucer) is a symbol of the psyche. It corresponds to oneness, unity, and perfection. However, perfection is usually an accident when achieved on the physical plane. We are more likely to succeed in realizing our desire for wholeness when we accept and forgive the flaws, vulnerabilities, and frailties existing in ourselves, others, and the world at large.

The idea of wholeness reflects spiritual balance. Spirit exists in *all* forms. Our belief in UFOs can benefit us when we have a stable outlook regarding their place in the scheme of creation. These ideas can hurt us when we give them more influence over us than they deserve. The reality of a close encounter with a UFO may be traumatic or enlightening, or both, but so are the more common experiences of divorce, death, and disease. If UFOs act of their own accord to aid or abet our development as a species, we are ostensibly powerless to stop them to the extent that we are powerless to prevent famine, war, and pestilence.

Evolution is a tide washing over the shore of creation, even as a circle represents the cyclic continuum of all life. If life is eternal, then the attainment of wholeness and perfection is an ongoing process, beginning with the realization that we are stardust, we are the microcosm within the macrocosm, the vastness of space within human form.

---

5 Jung, Carl G., *Man and His Symbols* (New York, Dell Publishing Co., Inc., 1971), pp. 284, 285.

Whereas a certain amount of genuine, childlike naivete is necessary to make magic happen, abject phantasmagoric surrender does not help us, or anyone else, to get on with our business, or to love and share our love with all of life. In order that we may clearly identify the thunderbolts that hit us, we need to watch for fire falling from the sky with our minds and hearts open, and our Earth visions ready for the forge.

METEORITES AND MINERALS

Long ago the people of certain cultures believed the sky itself was made of stone. Australian Aborigines still hold to the belief that the sky is made of rock crystal and the heavenly throne of the Creator made of quartz.[6] As I have mentioned, rocks play an important role in the healing work of medicine people and shamans, for through the rock comes the mystic quality of heaven and the magic of space without time. In fact, it is the vast, cosmic timelessness inherent in rocks that allows the shaman to "see," with spirit eyes, far beyond the ordinary parameters of earthly vision.

It is easy to understand why primitive peoples believe that rocks come from the sky. For one thing, the Earth itself is a big rock spinning around in space. We don't often think of our home planet in this way; a more common perspective is that space is "out there" and we are here on solid ground. Before telephone, radio, and television, many eyes turned toward the heavens to see what was happening in the world. Beyond smoke signals and scouts, star-gazing was the only form of inter-global communication on planet. Primitive peoples could see stars, meteorites, and other heavenly bodies falling from sky to Earth, and thus receive "news" and even guidance for the future.

Meteorites were worshiped by primitive peoples all over the world, because the falling chunks of stone appeared to them as fire from the sky. Pieces of meteoric iron, or any part of the meteor,

---

6 Eliade, Mircea, *The Forge and the Crucible: The Origins and Structures of Alchemy* (New York and Evanston, Harper & Row, 1972), pp. 19–20.

were often said to be the Hammer of the Thunder God or a manifestation of the power of lightning.

In Norse mythology, Thor the Thunderer was the son of Odin, a shaman god, and Thor's mother was the Earth. The hammer was one of Thor's three prized possessions, along with the belt of strength, which enabled him to double his divine powers, and a pair of iron gloves to better wield the hammer. It is said that the Frost and Mountain Giants knew Thor's hammer well, as he threw it to cleave the skulls of many of their kindred. Yet the hammer always returned to Thor's iron-gloved hand when it was done waging battle. So the Thunder God's hammer *is* the lightning or the power of lightning, thrown down from the heavens to cleave the snow-capped mountain peaks (the Frost Giants' skulls). We might wax metaphoric and say that Thor's hammer is the electrical fire from the sky, charging the frozen water of Earth to reveal the bountiful mineral ores that were once heavenly bodies.

Vulcan, the son of Jupiter, a sky god, and Juno, a queen of heaven, was also a god of fire and a worker of metals. His workshop was beneath Mount Etna, where he forged thunderbolts for his father. Vulcan's nickname, the Softener, alludes to the metallurgic process of tempering metal (fire) with water until the desired shape emerges from the flames.

So a metalsmith is one who controls the fire from the sky. The work of metallurgy is done in the flames; therefore a metallurgist is a master of fire. A shaman is also a master of fire, but of the inner fire that breathes life and vitality into the spirits, gods, and the ailing human soul.

Alchemy comes out of the shamanic rituals or esoteric side of ancient smithcraft, in which abided the spirits of gods such as Thor and Vulcan. The alchemist also transforms physical substances and human energies from their original fire from the sky into more complex metaphysical structures. When we work with crystals, gems, and minerals, we too become masters of fire in the same way an old smith, metallurgist, or medieval alchemist was a master of fire.

NATURAL ALCHEMY

Nature is to humankind as humankind is to spirit. This idea, taken from an old alchemical axiom, tells us that humankind is the intermediary between Nature (the Earth Mother) and the sky (Sky Father), and that Nature and the sky are equal expressions of one polarity. If we look at the present state of the human condition, we can see that we are caught in an unending cycle of birth, marriage, divorce, disease, and death. By applying our mental fire to think, feel, and act upon natural principles and laws, it is possible to center ourselves within the turning wheel of life, and to fashion beautiful earth-forms that will truly embody our visions and desires.

Coming into balance with Nature and the sky is an alchemical process whereby the base metals or lower aspects of human personality may be dissolved, transformed, and returned to wholeness.

- Disintegration leads to integration.

- Transformation mediates between the two.

Through the alchemical process of transformation, our base metals—the instinctual urges over which we have no control—may be turned into gold, the union of personal mind, and the cosmos. This altered state of consciousness gives the alchemist (the smith, the shaman) the power to heal the Earth.

Many of us are interested in healing our own bodies, the body-earth. In fact, we cannot heal others until we are willing to be healed and restored to wholeness ourselves.

In ancient myth, it is the Bone Goddess who raises the dead. Whenever the Bone Goddess restores a body to life, she reconstitutes the cosmic human, or integrated personality. She may do so by singing an incantation, or by pouring the Water of Life and Death over the bones. In Mexican Indian lore the Bone Goddess takes the form of La Loba, the She-Wolf. She is an Animal Mother, sitting in a cave and pouring the Water of Life over the bones of various critters. A contemporary version of the myth has La Loba riding about in the back of an old Chevy pickup truck in search of roadkill to restore to life.

Likewise, the Water of Life is poured over Ishtar's bones in Sumerian myth, and in Russian faery tales the witch Baba Yaga provides the Water of Life which is poured over a person's bones. In the Finnish *Kalevala*, restoration is accomplished with an incantation, and when Egyptian Isis restores Osiris, she also sings an incantation.

There was an old tradition in Egypt, during the Greek and Roman period, that when Isis brought Osiris back to life she was acting as the first alchemist. (In those days one could find an alchemical text called *The Book of Isis*.) However, beyond the incantation, we might think of the magical elixir, the Water of Life, in these terms: the elixir is sometimes a healing potion and sometimes a deadly poison. When it is a deadly poison, the Water of Death, it is guarded by a dragon. It is also said that Baba Yaga takes the form of a great serpent, and wraps herself around the Water of Life and Death. In other words, the old Bone Goddess, whether La Loba, Isis, or Baba Yaga, was the first alchemist. When she removes the Water of Life from the bosom of the cosmic serpent and transforms the poison into a healing elixir, or when she works through incantation and the power of sound, she is acting as the alchemist, restoring the cosmic human to life.

Thor, as a god of lightning, uses his power (the hammer) to slay the dragon (the Bone Goddess) who is the keeper of the Water of Life and Death. The Thor myth teaches us that to slay the primordial dragon is to release the power of the Water of Life, the healing elixir that is the cosmic medicine.

In alchemical terms, restoration and transformation are the means whereby we become the living Stone of the Wise, a whole person. The divine operations through which we are able to accomplish this end include the following energies:

- The element of Air, transparency, Mercury, or Mind as the mediating agency.

- The element of Fire, electricity, the Sun, or the Spirit as the healer.

■ The element of Water, magnetism, the Moon, or the Soul as the cosmic medicine or Water of Life.

The Healing Elements

The elements of Air, Fire, and Water are applied to heal the body-earth, properties that are synonymous with the alchemical principles of mercury, sulphur, and salt. This divine triad represents the union of mind, spirit, and body, and is associated with the following characteristics, constellations, and mineral ore equivalents:

Mercury is vital, intelligent, and transparent. The mutable constellations Gemini, Virgo, Sagittarius, and Pisces are mercurial in nature. Native Mercury (Quicksilver) is a heavy silver liquid having a low melting point, which enables it to merge into any shape and seep through every crack, crevice, and container except glass.

Sulphur is fiery and passionate, the first cause of activity and desire. The cardinal constellations Aries, Cancer, Libra, and Capricorn are sulfuric in nature. Native Sulphur, a mineral ore derived from volcanic gases, is known for its corrosive action when manufactured as sulfuric acid.

Salt is stagnant and inert, arrestive and binding. The fixed constellations Taurus, Leo, Scorpio, and Aquarius are salty in nature. Natural Salt is well known as a preservative as well as for its cleansing properties, having the rough, grainy texture of sand combined with strong anti-bacterial agents.

Salt contains many of the trace minerals necessary to sustain life. In fact, there are twelve trace minerals, known as tissue or "cell" salts, that are necessary to maintain balance and wholeness in the body-earth. The cell salts are vital components of the body, the workers and builders that combine with organic matter (the food we consume) in creating and maintaining the millions of cells in the body. Normally, these twelve elements are present in healthy blood and tissues. Any cell salt deficiency or imbalance may result in disease, the symptoms varying according to the salt which is lacking. By supplying the deficient cell salt to the bloodstream, the cells are returned to normal functioning, and health may be restored, a method akin to the practice of homeopathy, which effects a cure by infusing the body with a minute dose of the very substance that produces the condition of disease. One excellent source of cell salts may be found in fresh fruits and vegetables. Another is in crystals, gems, and minerals, because cell salts are actually mineral crystals in natural chemical form. In the following section is a list of constellations, minerals, and cell salts and their healing properties.

Mercury, Sulphur, Salt
The divine triad encompasses Mercury (top), Sulphur (lower left), and Salt (lower right), and their correspondences to the elements and the constellations.

THE CELL SALTS

Aries = Meta-Ankoleite = Potassium Phosphate

Potassium phosphate is a nerve nutrient, excellent for treating
headaches and eye fatigue.

Taurus = Thernadite = Sodium Sulphate

Sodium sulphate is a diuretic and helps to eliminate toxins from
the lymphatic system.

Gemini = Sylvine = Potassium Chloride

Potassium chloride aspirates the circulation, thereby conditioning
and purifying the blood.

Cancer = Fluorite = Calcium Fluoride

Calcium fluoride builds elasticity in the tissues and cells of
the body.

Leo = Newberyite = Magnesium Phosphate

Magnesium phosphate strengthens the muscle tissue of the heart
and stabilizes the central nervous system.

Virgo = Jarosite, Aphtitalite = Potassium Sulphate

Potassium sulphate promotes the flow of oxygen in the
bloodstream.

Libra = Stercorite = Sodium Phosphate

Sodium phosphate neutralizes acids through the functions of
the kidneys.

Scorpio = Anhydrite = Calcium Phosphate

Calcium phosphate purifies the blood and is an excellent tonic
for healing skin inflammations.

Sagittarius = Quartz Crystal, Cat's Eye, Tiger's Eye, Aventurine = Silica

Silica is an internal body cleanser.

Capricorn = Autunite, Apatite, Collophanite = Calcium Phosphate

Calcium phosphate is a general nutrient.

Aquarius = Halite = Sodium Chloride

Sodium chloride assists in distributing water throughout the body.

Pisces = Vivianite = Ferrum Phosphate

Ferrum phosphate carries oxygen throughout the body.

⇥ CRYSTAL MEDICINE 2 ⇤
STONE SEARCH

1. Learn everything you can about the primary mineral/cell salt associated with the zodiacal constellation under which you were born. If you are not sure what your primary mineral looks like, go to your local natural history museum or research a field guide to North American rocks and minerals.

2. Locate an actual specimen of the stone. New Age boutiques, gem shops, and flea markets are all good places to look.

3. Make or buy a pouch for your special stone. It is best that the pouch be made of natural materials, such as leather, silk, or cotton.

4. Talk to your stone as outlined in Crystal Medicine 3 in the next chapter.

5. Place your special stone in the pouch and wear it on or about your person.

3

THE CRYSTAL SYSTEMS

ARTH FATHER

Those who are familiar with the Tarot (a deck of seventy-eight pictorial cards designed to preserve and transmit spiritual teachings) will recognize The Hermit (the Earth Father) as the keeper of a six-rayed star.

The Hermit stands alone on a solitary mountain peak holding up a lantern through which shines the six-rayed star. He is a light bearer. The mountain is a metaphor for higher consciousness, and the star in his lantern is a guide for those who have yet to ascend the mountain.

The Hermit represents enlightened consciousness. Although he stands alone in the outer darkness, he carries the golden inner starlight, a symbol of natural principles and cosmic laws. The image of the Hermit intimates that as we deepen in our wisdom and understanding of Nature, the darkness recedes, and the light shines more brightly until we remember that spirit, soul, and matter are one, and we begin to act accordingly.

Alchemy uses the symbol of a six-rayed star to illustrate the creation of the Earth and its forms. This symbol is composed of two interlocked equilateral triangles. The descending triangle signifies

37

the element of Water and the involution of spirit energy into earth. The ascending triangle represents the element of Fire and the evolution of conscious awareness.

Together these triangles form a macrocosmic and microcosmic diagram of the awakening of human spiritual potential (the lightning bolt of Thor searing into the dense matter of Earth). The Water triangle reflects both the cosmic water surrounding the Earth and the "water" at work in the psyche, the subterranean level of the mind where our visions and dreams, instinctual urges, and emotions reside. The Fire triangle indicates heavenly fire as well as the fire at the Earth's molten core. It is also the inner flame that vivifies the mind, ignites the psychic depths of the unconscious, and initiates our dreams, visions, and impressions to action.

The Six-Rayed Star

This diagram illustrates the macrocosmic and microcosmic elements of the awakening of human spiritual potential, as the symbols for Fire and Water overlay the circle of Earth.

The earliest versions of The Hermit card are actually called *il Gobbo*, the Old Man. The figure carries Saturn's hourglass on his back, symbolic of the sands of time. In another old Tarot deck, The Hermit card is called "Cronico."

il Gobbo

CHAPTER 3

Cronico is Chronos,[1] the Greek equivalent of the Roman god Saturn and the common Greek word for "time." In myth, Saturn (Cronus) is described as a monster who devoured all his children. However, his sons Jupiter, Neptune, and Pluto escaped this fate. When Jupiter was grown, he asked Metis to give Saturn a draught to make him disgorge his other brothers and sisters. Jupiter, along with his newly liberated siblings, rebelled against Saturn. Upon dethroning their father, Jupiter, Neptune and Pluto divided his dominions among themselves.

Saturn the Devourer *is* Father Time, eating away at life and all its forms—creatures, things, ideas, and feelings. Time is chaos here on Earth because it is always moving, always restless, always breaking down order and matter. Yet time is also a continuum, an eternal cosmic flux and flow that devours the past to reveal future progress.

Sometimes Saturn is shown carrying a scythe, another symbol of devouring. The curved shape of the scythe corresponds to the feminine principle, which is why alchemists named Saturn Mercurius senex, i.e. "Mercurius, the Old Man." This title also gives him an ambiguous gender (because Mercury is androgynous) and relates him to the Earth.[2]

Western mythologies recognize the Earth as a woman. The thunderbolts and meteorites that cleave the Earth represent a sacred union between the male and female. Saturn in his guise as an Earth Father is therefore a consort of Mother Earth.

In Greek myth, Saturn was the son of Gaia, the Earth. Her womb, like the wombs of all Earth Mothers, symbolized the source of rivers as well as the cave, the cavern, and the mine. Because he was born of the womb of the Great Goddess Earth, Saturn also rules mining, according to ancient traditions.

Crystals, gems, and minerals are born in the womb of the Earth Mother. Metallic ores, coal, salt, precious stones, and other minerals are extracted from their birthplaces: caves, mines, or large exca-

---

1 Huson, Paul, *The Devil's Picture Book* (London, Sphere Books Ltd., 1972), p. 193.
2 Cirlot, J. E., *A Dictionary of Symbols* (New York, Philosophical Library, 1983), p. 278.

40

vations on the earth's surface. Everything that lies in the womb of the Earth is alive, even if only in a state of gestation. For the primitive miner, as for the alchemist, mining held many tenets of the process of transmutation, because both knew Nature, the Earth Mother, to be a living being.

If you have ever lived in the shadow of a mountain that has suffered from industrial strip mining, you already know it as a rape of the land for profit, and a curse on Nature and humankind. (I watched as a section of the Ortiz Mountains of north-central New Mexico was turned from a piñon-forested, snowcapped peak to a barren, erosion-prone wasteland by careless strip miners, and it was not a pretty sight.) Stones that sleep deep within the belly of the Earth are a form of *embryo*. Hidden in the dark places under the Earth, they grow and evolve according to their own time and ripen in due season, turning from ores to metals, such as silver and gold. To forcibly extract an ore before its time is to stop it from developing fully, for, like organic living beings, stones go through stages of evolutionary development, maturing, aging, and dying.[3] When the stones die, their spirit energy is released into the bodies of plants, animals, and elemental forms.

EARTH ELEMENTALS

Elves, gnomes, and dwarves are the elemental beings associated with the Earth. These mischievous spirits are easier to perceive than Fire, Water and Air elementals—salamanders, undines, and mermaids, and sylphs and giants, respectively. This is because earth elementals have a relatively dense electromagnetic composition compared to the others.

We are likely to run into earth elementals when out rock hounding. When they are hovering close by, we may experience minor physical mishaps, doubt, insecurity, or pettiness and greed, because they are very possessive and like to protect their own turf, especially crystals, gems, and minerals. However, these earth spirits are also guardians and protectors of humankind.

---

3 Eliade, Mircea, *The Forge and the Crucible*, p. 42.

The earth elemental is a source of power for shamans. Many North American Indian tribes speak of a "little green man," only two feet tall, who lives in the mountains, carries a bow and arrow, and is the guardian spirit of medicine men, or a dwarf who gives power and serves as a guardian spirit.[4]

STONE SPIRITS

Eventually, stone spirits incarnate into human bodies. Therefore, unlike contemporary mining companies and their workers, ancient miners and metallurgists assumed responsibility for their intervention in the birth processes of precious stones. They had full knowledge that they were superseding Nature by overriding time, but they did so with reverence. They were conscious of the limitations imposed by their own mortality. They were aware that by delving into the mysteries of the Earth they were tapping into the source of all life.

Solitary mining, provided it is done with respect for Mother Earth, is far less invasive to the land and Nature in general. Mining in this way requires only a few tools for gathering, labeling, and identifying specimens. As crystals, gems, and minerals grow in caves, quarries, old mining sites, river beds, and wild, mountainous regions, an expedition to find the perfect stone can lift us out of the ordinary environs of daily life and into the unpredictable domain of Nature. Beyond careful attention to weather, drinking water, snakes, and biting insects, a journey into the wilderness is a journey in search of the root of cosmic water, Earth Mother, Star Woman, all our relations, and our very own soul.

Long ago, back in prehistoric times, we began to change Nature. By so doing, we inadvertently took on the role of Father Time, because we no longer allowed Nature to take its own course in the seasonal procession of universal time. We decided when and if certain animals would be born, crops would ripen and be harvested, and minerals would be taken from their beds.

---

4 Eliade, Mircea, *Shamanism*, p. 102.

As we learned in chapter 2, one function of human consciousness is to assist the cosmos in creating earth-forms. We began doing this as soon as we hit two flints together and played with the resulting fire. Now our mastery of fire may be seen in the context of cultural progress as the origin of metallurgy, as well as in the physical and psychological techniques that formulate the basis for shamanism, alchemy, magic, science, and physics.[5] Therefore, it is important to recognize Fire and Water as the basis of our work with stones:

Fire is sacred. Its heat brings us closer to the gods and spirits, which is one reason Native Americans sweat in the rock-borne heat of the purification (sweat) lodge, and ancient Europeans perspired in their saunas. Nature is changed through fire. By aiding Nature, we work with the gods and spirits to bring about earthly perfection.

Nature is divine. Through Nature we seek perfection, transformation, the Stone of the Wise, the Water of Life. When we attempt to change Nature, we are really seeking to change and perfect ourselves that we may be divine also, free from the constraints and limitations of time. In this way, we are all shamans, metallurgists, smiths, magicians....When it gets right down to it, we are all alchemists.

CRYSTAL SYMMETRY

All matter in the universe is made up of atoms. Every earth-form has a basic atomic pattern that defines its inner structure and outer appearance. Atoms that form into crystalline substances vary in physical structure and external coloration. However, although crystals, gems, and minerals come in myriad shapes and sizes, there is always a strict symmetrical order to their basic atomic structure.

Crystals always grow in accordance with simple, mathematical laws. There are now six crystal systems that delineate their symmetry: Isometric, Orthorhombic, Tetragonal, Monoclinic, Hexagonal,

---

5   Eliade, Mircea, *The Forge and the Crucible*, p. 169, 170.

and Triclinic.[6] The stones listed below will differ from the traditional gemstone and astrological correlations because we are using the six crystal systems. (You will find a detailed listing of all the stones in the "Crystal Encyclopedia" in part 2, chapter 8 of this book.)

Crystallographers, those who have made a scientific study of the form, structure, properties, and classifications of crystals, can fit any crystal into one of the six basic crystal systems, and so can we. Following is a list of the six crystal systems and their astrological correspondences. Only a few of the many crystals that fit into these systems have been listed; all the crystals listed in each system can be used by any of the corresponding astrological signs.

THE SIX CRYSTAL SYSTEMS

System I: Isometric (or Cubic)

Isometric crystals are generally blocky or ball-like in form, having many similar, symmetrical faces. They characteristically form as cubes, octahedrons, and dodecahedrons, either single or in various combinations. The isometric crystal system is also known as the cubic crystal system.

Constellations	Planets	Examples of Crystals
Gemini	Mercury	Native Gold, Silver, Copper
Cancer	Moon	Platinum, Sodalite, Fluorite
Aquarius	Saturn/Uranus	Garnet, Lapis lazuli, Galena, Pyrite

System II: Orthorhombic

Orthorhombic crystals are generally short and stubby, with a diamond-shaped or rectangular cross section. They characteristically form as four-sided prisms, pyramids, and pinacoids (open forms comprised of two parallel faces).

Constellations	Planets	Examples of Crystals
Taurus	Venus	Sulphur, Cat's eye, Peridot
Leo	Sun	Topaz, Marcasite
Scorpio	Mars/Pluto	

---

6 Chesterman, Charles W. and Lowe, Kurt E., *The Audubon Society Field Guide to North American Rocks and Minerals* (New York, Alfred A. Knopf, 1978), p. 33.

THE SIX CRYSTAL SYSTEMS

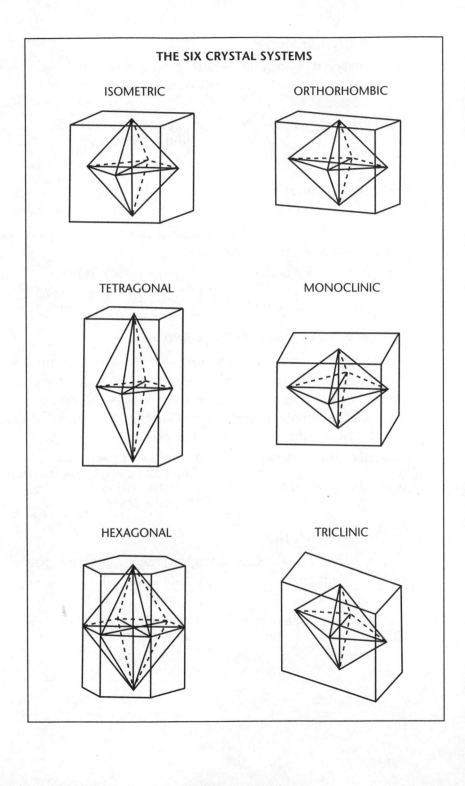

ISOMETRIC

ORTHORHOMBIC

TETRAGONAL

MONOCLINIC

HEXAGONAL

TRICLINIC

System III: Tetragonal

Tetragonal crystals are long, slender, or sometimes needlelike. They characteristically form into four-sided prisms, pyramids, and dipyramids.

Constellations	Planets	Examples of Crystals
Aries	Mars/Pluto	Rutile, Cassiterite, Apophyllite
Capricorn	Saturn	Zircon

System IV: Monoclinic

Monoclinic crystals are generally stubby, with tilted matching faces at opposite ends, suggesting a distorted rectangle. These crystals characteristically form as prisms and pinacoids.

Constellations	Planets	Examples of Crystals
Pisces	Jupiter/	Malachite, Azurite, Chrysocolla,
	Neptune	Jade, Selenite, Serpentine

System V: Hexagonal (or Trigonal)

Hexagonal crystals generally occur in prismatic or columnar formations, with rounded triangular or hexagonal cross sections. Characteristic hexagonal forms are three or six-sided prisms, pyramids, and rhombohedrons. The similar trigonal system is often included within the hexagonal system.

Constellations	Planets	Examples of Crystals
Virgo	Mercury	Tourmaline, Beryl, Quartz crystals,
Sagittarius	Jupiter	Cinnabar, Hematite, Calcite,
		Dioptase, Apatite

System VI: Triclinic

Triclinic crystals are flat with sharp edges and sharp, thin cross sections. No right angles occur on faces or edges. All triclinic crystal forms are pinacoids.

Constellations	Planets	Examples of Crystals
Libra	Venus	Turquoise, Wulfenite,
		Plagioglase Feldspars

◄ CRYSTAL MEDICINE 3 ► STONE SPIRITS

This two-part exercise will introduce you to the spirits and energies that live in Nature, as well as crystals, gems, and minerals.

Mining the Stone

1. Select a stone from the list on pages 40 and 42 that works with the constellation or planetary energy under which you were born—or let it be a stone that attracts your attention naturally and instinctively.

2. Learn everything you can about the stone you are seeking. Some specimens require only gentle brushing when found, while others may need careful trimming. Most minerals can be cleaned in water, but some will dissolve when wet. Also, some stones are affected by changes in temperature, pressure, and humidity, and so require special handling. Other stones will tarnish quickly in the open air.

3. Find out where the stone you have selected lives. Does it dwell in a cave, a stream, on a mountainside, in an abandoned mine? When you discover the place, make plans to go there for a day-trip or overnight, if necessary. Check to see if you need permission to harvest the stone in question in the area you have selected.

4. Meanwhile, gather the items you will need for harvesting your stone. Depending on the size and type of stone you are after, the essential items are a hammer or a geologist's pick, a small chisel, a prybar or crowbar, a pocket knife, a stiff brush, work gloves, an old newspaper, and a carrying bag. Bring goggles if you are mining quartz, because it shatters easily and cuts like a razor.

   Don't forget to bring mountain tobacco and an assortment of coins as offerings for Mother Earth. Mountain tobacco, a wild, naturally grown smoke, free of chemical additives, is used by Native and/or Pagan peoples for ceremonial purposes, as well as by smokers who realize that the chemicals used in the manufacture of commercially prepared cigarettes are the primary cause of smoke-induced disease, not the tobacco itself. You can find mountain tobacco at a local health food store or herb shop, or order it from a catalog specializing in American Indian products. The Earth spirits enjoy sharing in a good smoke now and then, and are revitalized by the dynamic energy vibration of the tobacco herb itself.

Coin offerings are very popular among indigenous peoples throughout the world. The theory behind a coin offering is that like attracts like. Money, and prosperity in general, is associated with the element of earth in many magical systems. By giving the Earth Mother a part of herself, she is satisfied and grateful.

5. If your search takes you to a quarry or mine, stay clear of loose boulders and beware of open shafts leading underground. If you are going into a wilderness area, be sure to first check the local conditions with hiking or mineral clubs, park rangers, etc.

6. Once you arrive at the cave, mine, or river bed, set all your equipment to one side, sit on the ground and ponder what you are about to do. Be aware of the sky above and the earth below. Talk to the gods and spirits of the place in your own words, telling them why you have come. Thank them for sharing their home with you. Then roll up some mountain tobacco in a cigarette paper and share a smoke, or leave a tobacco offering on the ground where you were seated.

7. Now, turn to the cave, mine, river bed, etc. and ask the Earth Mother permission to adopt one of her children, to remove one of her bones. Monitor the clouds in the sky, the wind in the trees, the movement of the water, the birds and wild creatures, and the sensations in your own body for the answer. If all seems gentle and mellow it is okay to harvest the stone. If the forces of Nature seem stirred up, or a part of

your body aches immediately after you ask the question, wait a while before asking again. It may take a little time for the Earth Mother to get used to the idea.

8. Once you receive permission, make a coin offering by leaving a few pennies, nickels, or dimes in the entrance of the cave or mine, or toss the coins into the river bed, if this is where your stone may be found.

9. Proceed with your harvesting, telling the stone all the while that you have come as a friend and protector.

Marguerite Elsbeth

A Rock Hound's Work Bench
This assortment of crystals, gems, and minerals lives at the home of Sherry Black and Everett Buss. Each stone was mined in solitary fashion.

CHAPTER 3

Stone Speak

1. Once you have harvested your stone, leave a pinch of tobacco in the hole you dug to remove it. Now sit down and carefully examine the stone. (If you are inside a cave or mine, go back outside before you do this.) Note its color, temperature, shape, and the sensation it produces as you turn it over in your hand. This is what a psychometrist does when handling an object in order to evaluate unseen radiations and impressions.

2. Close your eyes and ask the stone to tell you its properties, how it may help you, and what its special message is. If you think the stone may benefit you, ask permission to use it in the future.

3. Listen quietly for the answers to come. Do not be attached to the form in which the rock spirit speaks to you. The answers may come through sight, sound, touch, taste, smell, instinct, feeling, or the weather. Expect the unexpected.

4. Thank the rock spirit when you have received your answers.

4
SOUND AND LIGHT

SPIRIT ENERGY WAVES

Every physical form is a unique pattern, developed by electrical energy which permeates the atmosphere. Ancient alchemists and primitive shamans knew this to be true; however, quantum physicists only recently discovered that if matter is broken into smaller and smaller pieces (electrons, protons, etc.), it eventually reaches a point when it is no longer an object but a wave of energy. When matter is broken down again and again, it has no dimension and cannot be measured in earth terms.[1]

This might seem an astonishing theory to one whose consciousness is limited to outer appearances, but under such constricted mental conditions one sees what one expects to see. When our minds are open, anything can happen. We can expect the unexpected because we have eliminated the barriers created by shallow mental constructs. The world in which we live is no longer static when our thoughts, perceptions, and impressions are in synchronistic harmony with the cosmic rhythms of Nature and the Earth.

---

1   Talbot, Michael, *The Holographic Universe* (New York, HarperCollins Publishers, 1991), pp. 33.

Even more surprising than the fact that the universe is made of energy waves, there is evidence that indicates that the only time energy waves ever become matter is when we are looking at them! When we are not looking at them, they remain as waves of energy.[2] This latest finding reiterates what shamans and alchemists have known all along: *only conscious perception alters reality as we know it.* Nothing is static. The Earth is a vast sea of vibrating energy. Everything vibrates to the rhythm of the cosmos. The universe is alive and flexible, if we know when *not* to look.

Sound Vibration and Light

Vibration is sound. All creatures and things are created in, from, and through waves of sound and light. Sound and light waves result in electromagnetic currents. Electromagnetic currents radiate to all the directions of space and beyond. Part of electromagnetic currents is visible light, the light we can see with the physical organ of sight.

Electromagnetism is the product of an indefinable energy that underlies the physical forces of electricity, magnetism, light and heat. This energy was known as spiritual ether to the alchemists, *ain soph aur* or "the limitless light" to Qabalists, *prana* or *prakriti* to the Hindus, and "Great Spirit" or "Great Mystery" to the Native Americans. Herein I refer to it as "spirit energy."

Sound vibrations free up spirit energy with a sort of spiritual combustion not unlike physical combustion, which requires a burning chemical combination attended with heat and light. In the spiritual sense, our breath is charged with spirit energy; it carries heat and light, and this is why we are able to produce sounds and movement through our body. Our bodies are made up of electromagnetic currents and waves of sound and light.

There are also several scientific theories that explain the behavior of light:

- Light is reflected through the prisms created by the solid bodies of the stars and planets.

---

2   Ibid, p. 34.

- Light contains minute particles emitted from radiant bodies that travel through space.

- Light consists of waves traveling rapidly in ether, with a crosswise vibration at right angles to the waves' direction, then continuing in straight lines.

- Visible light is sometimes classified as electromagnetic energy occurring in waves shorter than infrared but longer than ultra-violet light, neither of which can be seen by the naked eye.

- Light is a form of radiant energy emanated from luminous heavenly bodies in tiny quantities called photons, which display both particle and wave behavior.

    This means that they have no charge or mass, but possess momentum. The energy that moves light is said to derive from photons.

Light Reflected through a Crystal Prism

However, whether the behavior of light is viewed from an eso-teric or exoteric standpoint, we find that the following holds true:

- Light disperses throughout the cosmos and pervades all of space.

- Everything is made from or is reciprocal with the electro-magnetic frequencies of which visible light is a part.

- Every substance in the universe is connected to light in its essential composition.

RAINBOWS OF COLOR

Sound is the wellspring out of which all forms originate. Color is the visual translation of sound. The form and movement of light waves vary as a result of the frequencies carried by sound. When this happens, light waves produce color. Color is the vibratory motion of refracted sound waves reflecting myriad forms of spirit energy to our field of perception.

There is a precise harmony between specific notes or tones cor-responding to the musical scale and the sum total of vibrations per second which transfer the *feeling* of a specific color to the sight cen-ter through the eyes. Also, the ears actually emit as well as receive sound, while the brain has a holographic way of processing sound.[3] This is why some visually impaired individuals can feel color, even though they can't see it, or why people who are deaf in one ear can locate the source of a sound without moving their heads.

The Body Prism

The human body radiates varying waves of light which correspond to the color spectrum from infrared to ultraviolet waves. The essen-tial wavelength of every cell and every organ within the body-earth has its own particular color and tone. When light passes through a prism such as is created by a clear quartz crystal, we can see a rain-bow of color. These colors are actual forces and have specific rela-tionships within the body-earth (see Color Wheel diagram, page 55).

---

3 Ibid, pp. 292, 293.

The human body is a prism also. When light passes in and through the body-prism, some individuals can see a rainbow of color called the *aura*. The aura is an etheric matrix consisting of seven distinct waves of light that surround the physical body. Sometimes the aura has the appearance of a luminous mist or cloud. It is possible to judge the condition of the body, mind, and emotions through the aura, because the aura radiates heat and light (electromagnetism) from the inner core of the body-earth, thereby displaying our life-essence. The aura grants us a visual picture of the level of electromagnetic energy generated from within the body.

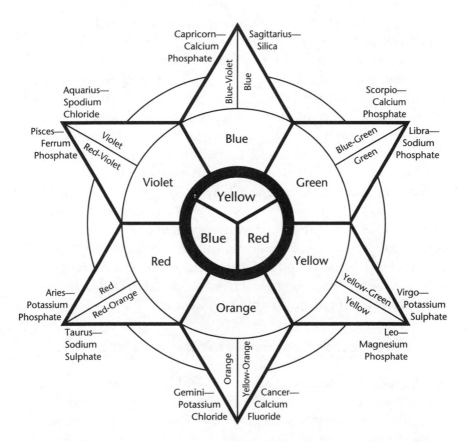

The Color Wheel

Specific relationships between colors, signs, and crystals are shown in this diagram. For more information, including sound, light, and elemental correlations, see pages 59–64.

This form of electromagnetic energy is produced by emotion. Magnetism and emotion are the same energies in different forms. Using the electrical currents of the mind to generate a magnetic/emotional flow of energy from within the body-earth is the basis of practice when working with crystals, gems, and minerals.

Body-Earth and Nature

All spiritual traditions have, at their core, a metaphor for bringing the auric life essence back into balance. As we have seen, in many ancient myths it is the Bone Goddess who raises the dead. In India the allegory is in rebuilding the dismembered body of *Prajapati* the Creator; in Qabalah, it's reconstituting Adam Kadmon, the primordial Adam or first man. In Egyptian myth the process entails the resurrection of Osiris by Isis, the first alchemist.

All of these traditions bring the body-earth back to Nature by raising the serpent power. This coiled serpent is the fire that lies asleep within the lowest body center, waiting to be awakened. In India, this system is called *Kundalini Yoga*. The Qabalists use a similar practice to build the Tree of Life within the aura. In Egypt, we have some fairly provocative evidence that there existed a meditative system in which the seven chakras—which we have defined in chapter 1 as "spirit energy centers"—were equated with the seven planets. There are interesting correspondences between Asiatic Indian concepts and the American Indian epic called *Popol Vuh*, where the Maya describe *kundalini* as lightning and depict body centers as animal instead of planetary energies. Awakening the serpent power is a means to attaining wholeness.

THE SEVEN SPIRIT ENERGY CENTERS

Just as our bodies are sensitive to heat and light, the food we eat, the air we breathe, and the environment, so are our thoughts, feelings, and actions prone to the influence of the aura, where the spirit energy centers reside. These centers are the guideposts of our inner natures. They let us know whether or not we are operating in consonance with our bodies and the world around us.

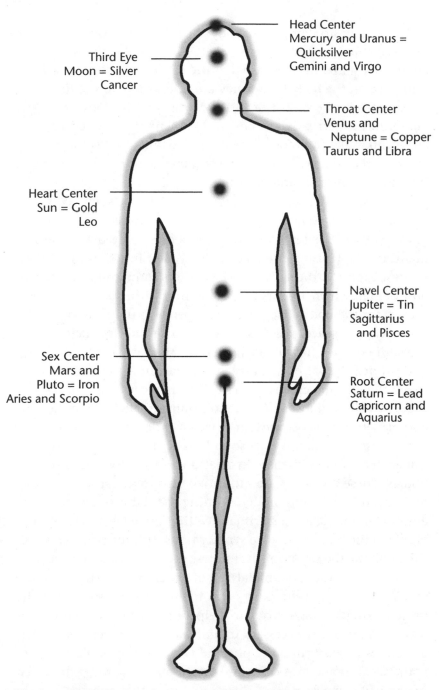

Third Eye
Moon = Silver
Cancer

Head Center
Mercury and Uranus =
Quicksilver
Gemini and Virgo

Throat Center
Venus and
Neptune = Copper
Taurus and Libra

Heart Center
Sun = Gold
Leo

Navel Center
Jupiter = Tin
Sagittarius
and Pisces

Sex Center
Mars and
Pluto = Iron
Aries and Scorpio

Root Center
Saturn = Lead
Capricorn and
Aquarius

The Seven Spirit Energy Centers with Planet and Mineral Correspondences
Often known as chakras, the spirit energy centers have a direct influence on the
body-earth, but are situated in the aura.

The atomic structure of the body-earth is constantly in a state of flux and requires a systematic intake, assimilation, and discharge of energy. As stated earlier, although the seven centers have a direct influence on the body-earth, they are not located in the flesh, but are situated in the aura. The auric body is the true body-earth, the blueprint or matrix that assimilates the energy supplied by food and drink. Like the Moon, the aura is a fluidic reflector of light from another source. Changes in the aura result from the vibratory influence of the stars and planets.

The seven centers are the energy at work in the spinal cord, the central nervous system, and the endocrine system in the body. They also serve as reservoirs from which we may draw nourishment and replenish our energy field. When functioning at their highest capacity, the spirit energy centers form a luminous rainbow of light which appears to radiate from within and extend outward from the body. Those who can perceive the aura say that it can occupy a space of several inches to several feet beyond the physical body of the average person. In the case of a highly magnetized or spiritual personality, the aura can actually expand to touch the infinite regions of space. This is because the aura is able to register the various frequencies of sound and light from the stars and planets in our solar system as well as from interstellar space.

Our responses to waves of sound, light, and color are based on the acuteness of our senses in relation to the physical and auric bodies. These responses are indicative of certain personal characteristics and are helpful in determining the status of our physical, emotional, mental, and spiritual health. The seven waves of light visible in the human aura are synonymous with the seven colors of the rainbow, the seven musical notes, the seven inner or "personal" planets and the seven metals, all of which have their root in the seven spirit energy centers. In order to enhance our work with the mineral kingdom as well as to help ourselves to remember our wholeness, it is first necessary to understand the seven spirit energy centers in relation to the physical body, the constellations and planets, colors and musical tones. Information regarding the seven metals will come later.

Before we begin, please keep in mind that there are numerous systems regarding the seven centers and color, and like snowflakes, no two are alike. Often we question which is the correct way of working with the centers. The answer is, there is no "right" or "wrong" way. All ways are good if they bring you to realize your wholeness. Therefore, if the bodily assignations, the constellations and planets, or the musical notes don't feel comfortable because they don't coincide with what you know, or for any other reason, then use the system that works for you. If the colors don't match your ideas and feelings, change them or use white, which carries within it the entire rainbow spectrum of color.

The Root Center = Saturn = Lead

The root center located at the base of the spine is also known as the sacral plexus. It is related to the element of Earth, and is associated with food, the material world, and the body-earth. This center governs the gall bladder, teeth, bones, sweat glands, knees, ankles, kidneys (via excretion), the lumbar region of the spine, and the vasomotor system.

Capricorn and *Aquarius,* the constellations ruled by the planets Saturn and Uranus (Uranus is the new ruler of Aquarius), are prone to afflictions that limit their mobility, such as mental/emotional oppression, broken bones, or diseases of the circulatory system. Capricorn may experience blockages involving career and reputation. Aquarian issues may involve friends, social groups, goals, and human fellowship.

Blue-violet, a mixture of red and blue, reflects gravity, excretion, the womb, and the ancestors. To some Native Americans, blue-violet symbolizes the thunderclouds and lightning, and the rain that cleans and refreshes the Earth Mother and her children. This color is both hot and cold. When balanced, blue-violet denotes practicality, sincerity, determination, perseverance, and good humor. Too much blue-violet makes for a cold, taciturn, suspicious, fearful, and retentive nature. When blue-violet is weak, inertia, insincerity, and a lack of discipline color the disposition.

A Natural, the musical note associated with the root center, is a strong, immunizing agent. Because it contains red, it is slightly stimulating. Use of the A Natural tone can aid in suspending tissue degeneration. It can be used to heal problems occurring in the skin, teeth, and bones, and is sometimes effective in healing stomach ailments.

The Sex Center = Mars and Pluto = Iron

The sex center located below the navel is also known as the prostatic ganglion, wherein lives the serpent power. It is associated with the spirit and vitality, the element of *Fire* in Western tradition, and *Water* in the East. This center governs the mesenteric plexi, the adrenal glands, the motor centers of the brain, the muscular system, the cells, and the reproductive organs.

Aries and *Scorpio*, the constellations ruled by Mars (Pluto is the new ruler of Scorpio), are subject to inflammatory and chaotic internal conditions, such as violent energy surges, headaches, sexually transmitted diseases, and sexual malfunctions. Aries may develop psychological symptoms pertaining to the ego and self-assertion. Scorpio issues may include sex, death, and power struggles.

Red, the first of the three primary colors, represents energy, strength, courage, activity, and endurance, because the blood coursing through our veins makes us feel alive. It is hot, vital, bold, and passionate. The lighter shades of pink and rose indicate healing medicine. A balanced amount of red denotes good sense, a clear and rational mind, and strong personal magnetism. When red is over-emphasized, the personality may be rash, angry, and hostile. Too little of the red vibration lowers vitality, causing fearfulness and feverish conditions.

C Natural, the musical note associated with the sex center, is a strong stimulant. Use of C Natural energizes the muscular system and warms the blood. It also stimulates sluggish circulatory and mental processes.

The Navel Center = Jupiter = Tin

The navel center or abdominal brain located in the sympathetic nervous system behind the stomach is also known as the epigastric ganglion or solar plexus. It corresponds to the elements of *Water* and *Fire* in the West, and *Fire* in the East, and is associated with feelings and the emotional plane. This center rules the coccygeal and sacral region of the spine, the iliac arteries and veins, the sciatic nerves, the femur, hips and thighs, feet and toes, and is active also in the stomach, mammary glands, and liver.

Sagittarius and *Pisces* are the constellations ruled by the planet Jupiter (Neptune is the new ruler of Pisces). Both suffer from mental and/or physical inactivity. When these temperaments lack a strong emotional support system, the result may be depression and excessive behavior, such as overeating, drug and/or alcohol abuse. Sagittarius may have issues with religion, education, and commitment. Pisces concerns may center on altruism and idealism.

Violet, a mixture of red and blue, symbolizes Nature, the instincts, and mental expansion. It is both warm and cool. In certain Native American societies, violet represents the setting sun and the rolling waves of the spiraling wind. A balanced amount of violet results in a steadfast, loyal, trustworthy, and honest disposition. When violet is too strong, the temperament tends to be outspoken, preachy, overly liberal, and dogmatic. A weak amount of violet makes for an emotional, insubstantial, and noncommittal personality type.

A Sharp, the musical note associated with the navel center, is antiseptic and regulative. This tone is a mild stimulant. It promotes the normal flow of fluids throughout the body, relieves congestion in the nerve currents, and is helpful when applied to the delicate membranes of the eyes, mouth, nose, and genito-urinary organs.

The Heart Center = The Sun = Gold

The heart center, located behind and a little above the heart, is also known as the cardiac ganglion. It corresponds to the element of *Fire* in the West and to *Air* in the East, and is the seat of intelligence and the mental plane. This center governs the heart and the sympathetic nervous system.

Leo is the constellation ruled by the Sun. Leo needs to slow down as it approaches middle age as well as maintain a healthy diet in order to reduce the risk of heart disease, back problems, and circulatory disorders. Creativity and children may be key issues in Leonine problems.

Orange, a mixture of red and yellow, symbolizes vitality, robust good health, generosity, and regenerative power. It is hot and dry, not quite as strong as the red vibration. When balanced in the body, orange brings creative self-expression, fluent communication, humor, organizational skills, leadership ability, and a generous spirit. When orange is over-emphasized, the personality may be pompous, overbearing, and egotistical. An insufficient response to the orange vibration may manifest as low self-esteem and lack of confidence.

D Natural, the musical note associated with the heart center, is a mild stimulant that is especially beneficial to the central nervous system. It promotes increased vitality and quick recuperation from mental fatigue.

The Throat Center = Venus and Neptune = Copper

The throat center, located in the area of the throat, is also known as the pharyngeal plexus. It relates to the elements of *Earth, Air,* and *Water* in the West, and to *Ether* in the East. It is associated with joy, ecstacy, and bliss. This center controls the thyroid and parathyroid glands, the kidneys, the thalamus, the sensory organs, the lumbar region of the spine, and the skin.

Taurus and *Libra* are the constellations ruled by Venus. Both Taurus and Libra are prone to overindulgence, generated by a peaceful though indolent nature. This can result in weight gain, causing depression and a lowered resistance to disease. Taurus may find the root cause of physical symptoms centered on resources, possessions, and value judgments. Relationships may be at the root of Libran difficulties.

Green, a mixture of blue and yellow, represents Nature and plant life in general. It is both cool and warm. A proper balance of green produces an artistic, creative, and harmonious personality. Too much of the green vibration results in a capricious, wasteful, indolent temperament. When green is weak, the disposition may be lazy, wanton, overweight, and subject to throat infections.

F Sharp, the musical note associated with the throat center, is a mild sedative and depressant. It promotes the physical relaxation necessary for mental workers, and is beneficial for creative and inventive activities. It also affects balance and poise in action.

The Third Eye = The Moon = Silver

The third eye, located between the eyebrows behind the root of the nose, is also known as the pituitary or postnasal ganglion. It is associated in the West with the element of *Water* and corresponds to intuition and wisdom. This center governs the stomach, the female mammary glands, the esophagus, the thoracic duct, the upper lobes of the liver, the lower lobes of the lungs, the diaphragm, the neck, palate, larynx, tonsils, lower jaw, ears, the atlas and cervical vertebrae, the carotid artery, and the jugular vein.

Cancer is the constellation ruled by the Moon. Irrational fears and emotions may create digestive and glandular problems for Cancer. Home, family, and security issues could be the cause.

Blue, the third of the three primary colors, symbolizes the universe, memory, the emotions, and habitual behavior. It is cold and depressive. Properly integrated, blue gives a strong sense of rhythm and movement, and a graceful, sensitive, considerate, compassionate personality. Too much blue causes depression, sadness, despair, and a distant emotional nature. When the blue vibration is weak, the temperament may be anxious, nervous, and fretful, and suffer from insomnia, metabolic imbalance, or severe mood fluctuations.

G Sharp, the musical note associated with the third eye, is a strong sedative and depressant capable of cooling the blood and soothing the nerves. Mildly antiseptic, G Sharp may be used to relieve pain, especially neuralgia, toothaches, and rheumatism. It may also assist in the treatment of disorders affecting the neurotransmitters of the brain, such as anorexia, bulimia, insomnia, panic, mania, obsession, and schizophrenia.

The Head Center = Mercury and Uranus = Quicksilver

The head center, located near the center of the brain, is also known as the pineal gland or conarium. It is associated in the West with the elements of *Air* and *Ether,* and corresponds to the intellect. This center governs the shoulders, arms, hands, lungs, the upper intestines, the circulatory system, and the central nervous system.

Gemini and *Virgo* are the constellations ruled by Mercury. These signs thrive on their nerves. There is a marked tendency toward mental and physical exhaustion, bronchial disturbances, and colon irritation. Neighbors, relatives, transport, communication, and education are key issues for Gemini. Virgo may look to work, obligations, and co-workers for the source of problems.

Yellow, the second primary color, is warm, though not soothing. Plains Indian cultures believe that yellow symbolizes the dawning of a new day, a time to let go of the past and begin again. A sufficient response to yellow tones the intellect and lends suaveness to speech as well as charm, charisma, and mental/manual dexterity to the personality. When there is too much yellow, the temperament is likely to be erratic, thoughtless, and shortsighted. An undeveloped response to the yellow vibration results in confusion, indecisiveness, and superficiality.

E Natural, the musical note associated with the head center, is both stimulating and sedative. It balances the finer functions of the brain, and may aid mental alertness, discrimination, and emotional equilibrium.

⇥ CRYSTAL MEDICINE 4 ⇤ SPIRIT ENERGY BODY

This exercise will familiarize you with your spirit energy body, or aura. It is important that you perform it regularly in order to become more attuned to the particular color that radiates in, from, and through your body-earth. This will enable you to change your auric resonance more easily, such as when you feel run down or when you perform healing work.

1. Find a comfortable spot where you can lie down. This spot can be anywhere—on the front lawn, the bed, or living room couch.

2. Close your eyes. Relax. Breathe deeply into your belly and exhale fully several times.

3. Become aware of your physical body, especially the borders surrounding the body, where the air and the skin connect.

4. Gently expand the borders as far as possible.

5. Now, within this expanded border, "see" the spirit energy radiating in, from and through your earth body. What color vibrates there? Is it bright or dark, light or heavy? Are there any areas in the spirit energy body that are dull, murky, or empty?

6. Sometimes it is difficult to envision the color of your spirit energy body. If the color is not clear to you, imagine white or silver-blue light, or pick your favorite color.

7. If there are dull or murky areas in your spirit energy body, brighten them up. If there are pieces missing, fill them in with spirit energy.

8. Ask your spirit energy body to tell you the meaning of the color you are or the color you have chosen. (Later, you may wish to use The Seven Spirit Energy Centers section as a guide to further assess the meaning of your particular color.)

9. Expand or shrink the borders of your spirit energy body to a comfortable size.

10. Open your eyes.

5

METALS

THE BIRTH OF METALS

Some cultures believe that stones engender human life. This idea occurs again and again in myths ranging from Central and South America, through the Near and Middle East, right down to the Pacific Islands. It arises from the energy put out by the stones themselves—real, solid, living, holy. Because they are incarnate in everything around us, many cultures venerate stones as an indestructible and absolute reality, the source of all life, and the very bones of Mother Earth.[1]

As we have seen, stones gestate in the belly of the earth. Precious gems and metals are born from strata, rock, clay, and dirt. However, the birth and growth of precious gems and metals in the earth demands a host. Long ago, this meant feeding the earth with blood to ensure fecundity and growth, so that the crops would ripen for the harvest.

Some Native American tribes tell the story of Corn Mother, who sacrificed herself and spilled her own blood on the rocks in the fields so that the crops would grow tall and the people would eat.

---

1   Eliade, Mircea, *The Forge and the Crucible*, p. 48.

In ancient Europe, the best horse in the countryside was sacrificed to ensure good crops. The creature was stabbed with a spear, and its head and tail cut off and adorned. These parts were then taken to the king's house and the blood from them allowed to drip into the stone hearth.[2]

In a similar vein, European shamans would pour blood onto the earth to call up the spirits of the dead, while some American Indian medicine men would feed their magic crystals the blood of an animal twice a year in order to keep the stones from flying through the air and attacking humans; once the crystals received blood to drink, they would fall into a contented and peaceful sleep.[3] Feeding blood to the earth or to certain crystals was a way of propitiating the spirits that dwelled in the Earth as well as in the stones.

Alchemical Traditions

In the Middle Ages, it was thought that ores were born by the union of the two alchemical principles, Sulphur and Mercury. (You will recall our discussion of these principles in chapter 2). In the union of Sulphur and Mercury, Sulphur behaved like the male seed and Mercury like the female seed. Together these substances conceived their metallic children—lead, tin, iron, copper, silver, and gold.[4]

Other alchemical traditions indicated that the stars controlled the reproduction of metals. For example, silver was said to grow under the influence of the moon, copper ore by the influence of the planet Venus, iron by the influence of Mars, and lead by the influence of Saturn.[5] Likewise, gold was born under the influence of the Sun.

As stated in a metallurgical and alchemical text from the late Middle Ages, *The Bergbuchlein*, the ancients taught that gold grew from a sulphur, "....the clearest possible, and properly rectified and purified in the earth, by the action of the sky, principally of the

2 Elsbeth, Marguerite, and Kenneth Johnson, *The Silver Wheel: Women's Myths and Mysteries in the Celtic Tradition* (St. Paul, MN: Llewellyn Publications, 1996).

3 Eliade, Mircea, *The Forge and the Crucible*, p. 45.

4 Ibid, pp. 47–48.

5 Ibid, pp. 48–49.

sun, so that it contains no further humour which may be destroyed or burnt by fire..."[6]

If nothing impedes the process of mineral gestation, in my opinion all ores have the capacity to become gold in time. All crystals, gems, and minerals evolve into metallic forms. For this reason, mines were once allowed to rest after an active period of exploration: the Earth needed time to grow more stones and mineral ores.

Mineral Maturation

In the maturation of minerals, the diamond is distinguished from the quartz crystal as having greater evolutionary development; the diamond is ripe, while the quartz crystal is still in matrix. Some gems and minerals have a different color when they are grown than at the time of their birth. The ruby is a prime example of this behavior; it begins as a white-colored stone and gradually turns red with age.[7]

Crystals of a metal may be grown in a laboratory setting using the method below.

☠ CAUTION: The following process will expose the user to mercury (quicksilver), which medical authorities warn is highly toxic to breathe, touch, or ingest. See pages 74–75 for more details on the risks involved.

Get a test tube. Put a drop of mercury (quicksilver) in a solution of 0.5 g. of silver nitrate in 20 cc. of water. Some of the mercury goes into the solution, liberating metallic silver, which combines with the remaining mercury to form a crystal alloy. The blade-shaped crystals will continue to grow for about a week.[8]

PRACTICAL ALCHEMY

Metals are the top of the line in the scheme of crystal evolutionary development, and gold is the apex of development in the mineral kingdom. Therefore gold represents the highest state of spiritual perfection one can reach when working with practical alchemy.

---

6   Ibid, p. 49.

7   Ibid, p. 44.

8   Holden, Alan, and Phylis Singer, *Crystals and Crystal Growing* (New York, Anchor Books, 1960), p. 122.

CHAPTER 5

The idea of alchemy might be a turn-off if we think of it only as a confused and early form of chemistry practiced in Renaissance Europe. However, if we think of alchemy in the broader sense, as the art of magical transformation through working with crystals, gems, and mineral ores from the Earth, then we have an entirely different perspective on the subject.

Alchemy is usually interpreted in one of two ways. The first theory holds that the alchemist works in a laboratory setting, testing and trying base metals in order to create gold, the perfect metallic substance. The second equates the alchemist's laboratory with the human body, the base metals with the dross of human personality, and gold with salvation and enlightenment, the Stone of the Wise. I believe the practicing alchemist does both. He or she works with Nature to bring about earthly perfection, while at the same time working toward self-transformation and integral wholeness.

The alchemical process includes four stages, which are symbolized by four different colors:

- Black, representing primal matter, the ancestors, the soul.

- White, representing the initial stages of transmutation, purity, and mercury or quicksilver.

- Red, representing motivation, will, passion, and sulphur.

- Yellow, representing perfection, spiritual attainment, union, and gold.

The alchemical work also includes seven stages or operations through which wholeness is perfected:

1. Calcination, the death of all desire and interest in the material aspects of life.

2. Putrefaction, a process resulting from calcination and consisting of discrimination and separation following the destruction of matter.

3. Solution, wherein all remaining matter is cleansed and purified.

4. Distillation, the elements remaining from the process of solution.

5. Conjunction, the union of opposites, such as masculine and feminine forces.

6. Sublimation, suffering as a result of detachment from the world, and/or as a result of living a life dedicated to spiritual purposes while remaining in the world, in the body-earth.

7. Philosophic congelation, the fixation of volatile elements into a whole, i.e. the coming together of male and female elements in the production of a third and distinctly separate element, the whole person.

These seven stages were observed and experienced in the visions of Zosimos of Panopolis, an important alchemist of the third century A.D. In his waking dreams, he saw an inner, Otherworldly sanctuary where he was drawn to submit willingly to physical, emotional, mental, and spiritual torment. Zosimos stood before a priest who pierced his body through with a sword and slowly dismembered it. Then the skin of his head and face was flayed away and mingled with his flesh and bones. These parts were burned in a fire until Zosimos perceived the transformation of his body, and knew that he had become spirit. In a subsequent vision, Zosimos was once again dismembered by the sword-wielding priest; however, this time his body was boiled in a cauldron of water, "the liquid in the art of metals," until Zosimos finally became a spirit in body, mind, and soul, as well as a guardian of spirits.[9]

First Zosimos was burned in the fire, stripped of the poison of his outworn habits and misconceptions, the poisonous Water of Death. Then he was boiled in a cauldron of water—the magical elixir, the Water of Life. Thus Zosimos was brought back to life in spirit. His spirit was renewed, cleansed, purified, refreshed.

In essence, the entire alchemical operation is reflected in the following formula: analyze the physical, emotional, mental, and spiritual aspects of being; submit to a greater force or entity; break down negative and inferior habits, thoughts, and feelings even though what is known and familiar also breaks down; and then reconstitute the remains into a whole and perfected personality.[10]

9 Jung, C. G., The Collected Works of C. G. Jung: Volume 13, Alchemical Studies (Princeton: Princeton University Press, 1976), pp. 59–65.

10 Cirlot, J. E., A Dictionary of Symbols, pp. 6–8.

Zosimos did not undergo transmutation alone, nor did he direct the entire alchemical process himself. A priest appeared in his vision to help him out. Zosimos' place was to accept torment and remain alert through his pain. Therefore, the operative phrase in the above synopsis of the alchemical process is *submit to a greater force or entity*. The Great Work of transmutation cannot be accomplished unless we willingly, consciously acknowledge a spirit greater than ourselves as the guiding presence in all our actions. The Great Spirit performs the actual work of alchemy, and we assist Nature in the sacred journey home.

Shamanic Practices

The Yakut people of Siberia say: "Smith and Shaman come from the same nest"....the smith is the older brother of the Shaman."[11] That alchemy has its roots in both metallurgy and shamanism can readily be seen in the rituals accompanying shamanic initiation.

The South American Cobeno shaman put rock crystals into the head of his apprentice so that the crystals could eat out his brain and eyes and take the place of those physical organs to become the apprentices' power and strength.[12] Among the Wiradjuri tribe of Australia, the initiate received rock crystals into his body and was made to drink water in which crystals had been placed (the magical elixir or Water of Life). Once he drank the living crystal water, the initiate began to see spirits.[13]

The Aranda tribe of Central Australia had a method whereby they initiated medicine men "by the spirits." The prospective medicine man went to a cave entrance and fell asleep. A spirit came and threw an invisible spear at him, which pierced his neck, passed through his tongue and flew out through his mouth. Another spear was cast, cutting off the candidate's head. The spirit then carried the helpless candidate deep into the cave to the Aranda Otherworld, a paradisical place of perpetual light. Once sheltered inside the cave, the spirit ripped out the candidate's internal organs and replaced

---

11 de Santillana, Giorgio, and von Dechend, Hertha, *Hamlet's Mill: An Essay on Myth and the Frame of Time* (Boston, Gambit Incorporated, 1969), p. 128.

12 Eliade, Mircea, *Shamanism* (Princeton, Princeton University Press, 1964), p. 52.

13 Ibid, p. 135.

them with organs that were new and improved. These new organs were actually quartz crystal fragments put into the medicine man's body by the spirit. Possession of these crystals gave the newly initiated medicine man his power.[14]

Initiatory Methods

As we can see, the alchemist's body is gifted with the most precious of metals—gold, or the Stone of the Wise—while the shaman's body is filled with quartz crystal, granting him or her spirit eyes to see into the Otherworld. Both initiatory methods require a complete personal makeover of body, mind, and soul. Each way brings the personality to realize increased spiritual awareness and integral wholeness of being through the use of metals and stones.

THE SEVEN METALS

Alchemy employs seven metals, each one associated with the seven colors of the rainbow as well as the seven spirit energy centers. These metals represent actual physical substances in the body as well as aspects of the mind and emotions.

Gold

Crystal System: Isometric

Properties: A native ore with some silver, copper, and iron

Colors: Gold-yellow, brass-yellow, and pale yellow; highly metallic; does not tarnish

Gold energy extends awareness and alters our perceptions with love. Its influence is regenerative, dynamic, and projective. Gold is a malleable transmitter of spirit energy that excites the masculine aspect of human nature. When used as a tool for meditation, gold directs the stream of cosmic substance that originates in the spirit world to flow into the field of human sensory experience. In healing work, gold energy initiates and motivates the patient to wellness. Gold is a very powerful metal. It must be used wisely and

---

14 Ibid, pp. 46, 47.

worn with great care. Because of its beautiful yellow luster and potent healing energy, gold has been used for many diverse purposes over the centuries, and will continue to be a primary metal resource for future generations. All crystals, gems, and minerals are compatible with gold ore.

Silver

Crystal System: Isometric

Properties: A native mineral ore, often with much gold or
   mercury, and lesser amounts of arsenic and antimony

Colors: Silver-white or tarnish yellow

Silver energy is feminine, watery, reflective, and introspective. This metal enhances our ability to be receptive and intuitive as well as to remember our wholeness. Silver's subtle and suggestive magnetic energy field makes this metal an excellent conductor, medium, and channel for psychic awareness. Silver is safer than gold; wear it to maintain balance, and to bring soothing energy, coolness, and quiet to the personality. According to Edgar Cayce, the right mixture of silver and gold is extremely rejuvenating and may actually double the lifespan if used properly. Like gold ore, silver has been employed for a variety of uses, and will continue to grow in popularity for both men and women. All crystals, gems, and minerals are compatible with silver ore.

Mercury (Quicksilver, Cinnabar) ☠

Crystal System: Hexagonal

Properties: Quicksilver (native mercury) is a heavy, tin-white
   liquid; cinnabar, the principle ore of mercury, is comprised
   of mercury sulphide

Colors: Bright, purplish red to brownish red

Mercury is a neutral transmitter of spirit energy, especially when used in the form of quicksilver, a rare liquid usually occurring with cinnabar as heavy, tin-white metallic droplets.

☠ CAUTION: Mercury is a highly poisonous substance and difficult to obtain legally. It dissolves all known substances, including

74

gold, and must be kept in a fully sealed, thickly layered glass container, since glass is the only substance from which it cannot escape. It is dangerous to breathe, ingest, or even touch.

Superconductive mercury energy favors movement. Cinnabar and quicksilver are amplifiers; these metals will bring out the hidden side of human nature. Ancient Oriental magicians believed that powdered cinnabar crystals could be transformed into yellow-gold, and that eating from utensils made of the cinnabar-gold would bring long life. *(Editor's note: We now know that quite the reverse is true.)* Taoists thought of cinnabar as the embryo of immortality because they believed it was manufactured inside the body as sperm.[15] The brightest and clearest red cinnabar crystals are the strongest transmitters of spirit energy. Quicksilver should radiate a clear metallic silver color and be free from dirt and impurities.

Copper

Crystal System: Isometric

Properties: A native mineral ore often found with small amounts of arsenic, antimony, bismuth, iron, and silver

Colors: Copper metallic; may also be tarnish black, blue, or green

Copper energy affects the mind and emotions. It is especially useful in enhancing our ability to formulate clear mental images. Copper ore brings in love, affection, harmony, beauty, and peace.

When used for meditation, copper ore creates a reciprocal energy flow between the third eye and the navel centers, resulting in mental clarity and expansion. Copper is often used in jewelry, wands, and other magical instruments for transformation because it is an exceptionally good transmitter of healing energy.

Iron Ore (Hematite)

Crystal System: Hexagonal

Properties: Hematite, the principal ore of iron, is comprised of iron oxide

Colors: Steel-gray, red, reddish brown, black cast

---

15 Eliade, Mircea, *The Forge and the Crucible*, p. 112.

Iron, and hematite, the principal ore of iron, affect activity in the reproductive areas, exciting the energies necessary for procreation. This metal is a strong grounding influence for the atomic body. Moroccans consider iron a great protection against demons: a knife or dagger made of the metal is often placed under a sick person's pillow. Iron assists in sublimating the sex drive, and absorbs negativity on contact. Owing to its weight and density, iron/hematite helps us to focus spirit energy in the body-earth.

Tin (Cassiterite)

Crystal System: Tetragonal

Properties: Cassiterite, the principal ore of tin, is comprised of tin oxide, often with some iron

Colors: Brown or black

Tin, and cassiterite tin, have reached a plateau in evolutionary development; however, they will soon resume their movement and rebirth underground to clarify their dull luster. This metal affects prosperity and growth, and is mildly stimulating. Native tin can be used to ease passive-aggressive behavior patterns, and to bring about material, emotional, mental, and spiritual increase.

Lead (Galena) ☠

Crystal System: Isometric

Properties: Galena, the principal ore of lead, is comprised of lead sulphide

Colors: Dark lead-gray

Lead, and galena, the principal ore of lead, transmit sound and light frequencies. They assist in stabilizing the mind and bring thoughts back into focus. Native lead teaches us acceptance of our limitations.

☠ **CAUTION: Lead should not be handled or held next to the skin due to its toxic nature.**

However, beautiful, perfectly shaped cubes of galena crystal represent the human body in microcosm and may be employed for the purposes of physiosynthesis and reintegration.

NEW MILLENNIUM METALS

We are all concerned with the use of nuclear weapons. Nobody wants a nuclear power plant in his or her neighborhood, but as we only make noises in protest, there is currently no relief from our government's persistence in creating more radioactive waste. Perhaps it is best to view nuclear energy from a different perspective.

Following are the metallic energies that comprise the living core of nuclear power:

- Uranium, a hard, heavy, radioactive substance found only in combination with other mineral substances.

- Neptunium, produced by the irradiation of ordinary uranium atoms with neutrons; it does not occur naturally on Earth.

- Plutonium, a radioactive element that is obtained by bombarding uranium with neutrons.

Uranium, neptunium, and plutonium are, of course, highly dangerous and illegal substances. We are unable to acquire them, but these metallic elements might merit further investigation to ascertain what benefits could be gleaned through their sound ecological use. If you wish to work directly with similar metallic nuclear energies, uraninite, platinum, and sulphur may be safely and legally used instead.

Uraninite

Crystal System: Isometric

Properties: Uraninite is comprised of uranium oxide, often with substantial amounts of thorium

Colors: Uraninite is green to green-black with a brown-black, gray-black or olive-green streak

Planet/Constellation: Uranus/Aquarius

Elements: Ether, Air

Spirit Energy Center: The head center

Uraninite is an initiating substance that promotes ecology and conscious integration of the heart and mind. The radioactive properties inherent in the stone strongly influence mental activity toward humanitarian pursuits.

Platinum

Crystal System: Isometric

Properties: Platinum is a native ore with minor amounts of iridium, osmium, rhodium, and palladium as well as iron, copper, gold, or nickel.

Colors: Platinum is colored a shiny tin-white or steel-gray metallic. This metal does not tarnish.

Planet/Constellation: Neptune/Pisces

Element: Water

Spirit Energy Center: The throat center

The electromagnetic energy field of platinum induces emotional refinement and assists in cleansing impurities from the aura. It opens our consciousness to the idea that we are not our body, but auric beings comprised of fire from the sky. Platinum is compatible with all crystals, gems, and minerals.

Sulphur

Crystal System: Orthorhombic

Properties: Sulphur is a native ore which may contain small amounts of selenium. This non-metallic ore sometimes forms as a result of acid water on metallic sulphates such as gypsum and barite.

Colors: Sulphur crystals may be yellow, greenish, or reddish yellow, brown, or gray.

Planet/Constellation: Pluto/Scorpio

Element: Fire

Spirit Energy Center: The sex center

Sulphur regenerates the mind and emotions, and may assist in altering the atomic structure of the cells in the body. Because it incites consciousness to relinquish useless patterns of activity, sulphur may bring about extreme transformation and change. Bathing in sulphur hot springs is an excellent way to soak up this rejuvenating mineral element (see Appendix). The soft, translucent sulphur crystals are capable of transmitting an inexhaustible supply of vital cosmic energy to the body-earth.

HEALING WITH METALS

Metals and gemstones should be placed in contact with the skin when treating a specific problem or illness. When metals are applied in this way, they induce an electromagnetic influence on the cells and organs of the body. For example, by wearing a ring made of silver and tin one may calm the nerves and settle digestive disturbances as well as heighten instinctual perception. If a metal is to be worn in a ring, wear it on the finger corresponding to the spirit energy center associated with your Sun-sign, or on the finger

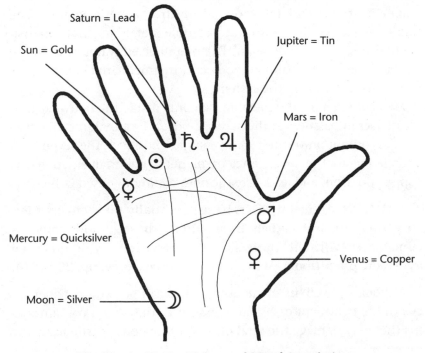

The Hand with the Planet and Metal Associations

associated with the constellation or planet relating to your emotional or physical discomfort (also see Spirit Energy Centers diagram on page 57).

☠ CAUTION: Do not place quicksilver (mercury) or lead on the skin, as these metals are extremely toxic.

TINCTURES AND ELIXIRS

Tinctures and elixirs containing gemstones and metals were used by shamans, Chinese alchemists, and most likely by Western alchemists as well. Contemporary New Age health marketing groups currently process a full range of liquid solutions, some of which contain metals such as colloidal silver.[16] However, the best surviving example of this tradition is in the Ayurvedic medicine of India, where such formulas are still commonly used for healing purposes.

A metal elixir is made by suspending in a fluid, such as distilled water, a small particle of the metal to be used. Because the water is magnetic, the metal takes on an electromagnetic charge. The resulting elixir is filled with water-soluble metal ions that can easily enter into the bloodstream. The metallicized water mimics the fluids of the healthy human body and the medicinal elixir is thus easily introduced into the system.

Metal elixirs take the metallic elements inside the body-earth to counteract imbalances of the body, mind, and soul. All metallic substances contain powerful healing energies; however, the seven metals relating to the seven ancient planets—gold, silver, mercury, copper, tin, iron, and lead—are the ones commonly used in healing.

☠ CAUTION: All metal elixirs have potentially toxic effects. Mercury, iron, tin, and lead elixirs should not be used under any circumstances without professional supervision by a qualified ayurvedic practitioner (see Crystal Resource Guide, pp. 209–210).

Although the elixirs made from metals can be extremely beneficial in the treatment of certain conditions, they often contain toxins that may damage the vital organs of the body, particularly the

---

16 Distributed by Oxygen for Life, Inc. (see Addendum).

heart, liver, spleen, and kidneys. The metals must therefore be purified before they can be used in a medicinal way. Ayurvedic physi-
cians will cure the metal to be used for healing by heating and/or
treating it with oil, cow's urine, milk, ghee, buttermilk, or the sour
gruel of grains to remove the poisons.[17]

Following are several recipes for metal elixirs. (Please refer to
chapter 4: The Seven Spirit Energy Centers, for a complete listing of
the body organs and conditions affected by the seven metals.)

Gold Elixir

Gold Elixir strengthens the heart and nerves, and is helpful for
those who suffer from a sluggish metabolism. Individuals with high
blood pressure, hypertension, irritability, or anger, or those who are
allergic to gold, may break out in a rash from gold elixir.

To make gold elixir, you will need:
    1 small piece of high quality gold (without a stone setting,
        if you are using jewelry)
    2 cups of purified water

Place the gold in a glass or stainless steel pot (do not use aluminum) with the water. Bring the water to a boil. Continue to boil
the water until half of the liquid evaporates. Take one teaspoon of
gold elixir two or three times a day, depending on the severity of
the condition.

Silver Elixir

Silver Elixir is soothing, cooling, and very helpful for mood swings
and digestive disorders. Silver elixir should be used sparingly by
individuals who are overweight or have a sluggish metabolism. It is
beneficial for those who are high-strung or overly aggressive in temperament. Silver elixir is prepared in the same way as gold elixir,
using silver in place of gold.

Another beneficial silver tonic can be prepared as follows:
    1 cup of milk
    A silver cup

17 Lad, Dr. Vasant, *Ayurveda: The Science of Self Healing, A Practical Guide* (Santa Fe,
    Lotus Press, 1984), p. 142.

Warm the milk in a glass or stainless steel pot. Pour into the silver cup and drink before bedtime.

Mercury Elixir

Mercury Elixir stimulates the mind and memory, and is helpful in treating upper respiratory conditions. Mercury elixir should never be used alone, but always with sulphur, which acts as a catalyst in bringing about fast relief of mercury disorders.

☠ **CAUTION: Ingesting mercury can be fatal.**

Copper Elixir

Copper Elixir is a rejuvenating mental/emotional stimulant, helpful in treating sore throats, nervous conditions, and temperaments prone to worry. A copper bracelet may be worn on the upper arm.

To prepare copper elixir, you will need:
    10 copper pennies
    Lime juice (bottled or fresh)
    1 quart of purified water

Wash the ten pennies in the lime juice. Place the pennies and one quart of purified water in a glass or stainless steel pot. Boil until half the water remains. Take two teaspoons of copper elixir three times a day for one month, or until the condition improves.

Iron Elixir

Iron Elixir conditions and strengthens the blood and muscular system, and may be effective in the treatment of anemia.

Tin Elixir

Tin Elixir is regulating and sustaining, and may be used along with a sensible diet and exercise plan to induce weight loss.

Lead Elixir

Lead Elixir aids concentration, and is good for treating problems relating to the skin and bones.

☠ **CAUTION: Lead is extremely toxic. Ingesting it is not advised.**

⇥ CRYSTAL MEDICINE 5 ⇤
SUN AND MOON WATER TONIC
FOR WHOLENESS OF BEING

Tonic waters containing the energies of the sun and/or moon embody very powerful healing benefits, and carry the same healthful properties as do gold and silver. While metal elixirs are potentially toxic and should be used only to resolve specific health problems under careful guidance and direction, sun and moon waters are perfectly safe and may be taken on a daily basis to bring about integral balance and wholeness throughout the body, mind, and soul. Clear quartz crystal catalyzes the absorption of solar and lunar energies as well as amplifies the healing benefits of the tonic water.

To prepare the following recipes for sun and/or moon crystal water, you will need:

    1 clear quartz crystal, cleaned and programmed
      (see chapter 6)
    Purified water
    A clear glass or bowl

NOTE: Both recipes should be prepared during a waxing moon phase.

To Prepare Sun Water

1. Wait for a sunny day, preferably on or right after the new moon. Put your crystal in the glass and cover with one cup of purified water.

2. Check an almanac (see Addendum) for the exact time of sunrise on the day you have chosen. At dawn's first light, place the glass out of doors in a sunny place (cover the glass with clear plastic wrap) or indoors on a sunny window sill.

3. Remove the glass at sundown. The water is now filled with the potency of the daystar. Drink sun water every evening to prepare the body for the rejuvenation process that takes place while you sleep.

To Prepare Moon Water

1. Wait for a clear night, preferably on or right before the full moon. Put your crystal in the glass and cover with one cup of purified water.

2. Check an almanac (see Addendum) for the exact time of sundown on the day you have chosen. At sundown, place the glass out of doors in a moonlit place (cover the glass with clear plastic wrap) or on a moonlit window sill indoors.

3. Remove the glass at dawn. The water is now filled with lunar potency. Drink the moon water every morning to prepare your body, mind, and spirit for the stress of the day.

Sun and Moon Waters
These waters, easily prepared, are beneficial tonics for the body.

6

MEDICINE HEALING FOR THE BODY EARTH

CRYSTAL MEDICINE WORK

Native American medicine people and healers from other tribal and shamanic cultures all over the world use stones and crystals when doctoring patients. Native peoples consider all rocks and stones sacred because they come from the Earth. We, too, need to view the mineral kingdom in this way, if we are to be in harmony with the energies flowing in on the tide of the New Millennium. While many beautiful mineral specimens are available, the most simple, ugly little pebble is a living stone spirit with special healing powers.

How we use stones for medicine depends on how the Great Spirit tells us to use them. Each stone possesses its own power, but the main consideration goes back to the shaman or healer: what properties does the medicine worker feel the stone possesses? How does the stone work for the healer as an individual?

There was once a time when arrowheads, usually cut from volcanic glass (obsidian), flint, or from metals such as copper or bronze in the case of ancient European shamans, were used by hunters and warriors. Today some Native American healers use arrowheads to hunt and kill sickness, to point out the location of the illness, or to send healing energy back into the body.

Lava rocks are used for heating the Native American sweat lodge because they sustain fire. Lava rocks are *wakan*, holy; they are the Grandfather rocks. When a person sweats in a sacred way, in the darkness of the womb of Mother Earth heated by glowing red lava rocks, sickness may leave the body and be dissolved in the steam and smoke. The person leaves the sweat lodge in a better way— healthy, whole, and renewed.

Holy Dance, a Sioux medicine man, found his magic healing stones. These two stones, which glow in the dark (possibly due to a high radium content), are used to heal muscle and bone troubles, as well as strokes. Holy Dance places the stones and his hand under hot water, and then puts them on the part of the patient's body holding the sickness. Residue from the stones boiled in water produces a curing tonic for the common cold.[1] In some Navajo and Shoshone medicine rituals, turquoise and jade are held together under water to send prayers to the Great Spirit to heal the patient's mind or body. When stones are placed under water and certain words are spoken, healing can happen.

Some Native American healers believe that silver and gold possess green energy, the power to make money. I know a Navajo-trained Shoshone-Bannock medicine man, a magnetic young man named Robert Perry, better known as Dude, who once employed turquoise and a half-breed coyote to manifest five thousand dollars. I'm not sure how he did it or even if it worked, but I don't think he held the stone and the critter under water for this one.

While all stones are sacred, crystals are usually the stone of choice to divine physical, emotional, mental, or spiritual problems, because as Dude says: "The crystal is like an x-ray machine; it allows the medicine person to see sickness inside the body." Crystals may be used in medicinal tonics or as surgical instruments as well. One Ecuadorian shaman from the Andes mountains uses a clear quartz crystal to draw sickness out of the body.

---

1 Lewis, Thomas H., *The Medicine Men: Oglala Sioux Ceremony and Healing* (Nebraska, University of Nebraska Press, 1990), p. 130.

Several years ago, I was on the receiving end of a Navajo-Shoshone crystal medicine healing. In fact, this is how Dude and I met.

Dude and his assistant had set up shop in a downtown Santa Fe apartment. (There's a lot of call for healing in Santa Fe.) When I arrived there was a line of prospective patients waiting on the landing outside. I was ushered into the front room, where a fire blazed in the kiva fireplace, even though it was a warm, late summer morning. Dude and I conducted a brief discussion over the blaring sound of the television. Once Dude had ascertained that I was there for healing, he instructed his assistant to gather coals from the fireplace. Dude asked me to wait and disappeared into a small back room. A few minutes later I was led into the room by Dude's assistant, who carried in a blackened aluminum baking pan the glowing coals he had gathered. (No fancy abalone seashells for them!)

I sat cross-legged on the floor facing Dude. The room was so thick with sage smoke that I could barely see him although he sat only two feet away. The assistant set the pan containing the coals down on the Navajo rug spread on the floor between us, and left Dude and me alone. I watched carefully as Dude rummaged through an old, battered briefcase, from which he retrieved a huge, clear quartz crystal and an eagle feather. He sprinkled more sage on the coals, fanned them with the feather, and began to chant and pray to the Great Spirit. As the coals glowed fiery red in the half-light and the room grew smokier still, Dude gazed at me through his crystal. He then proceeded to divine my problematical situation with great accuracy. Eventually he determined by looking through the crystal the part of my body that harbored the harmful spirit intrusion.[2]

Dude pierced my body with an eagle talon, and sucked out the spirit intrusion through a buffalo horn. The intrusion was a fragment of bone. The resulting wound bled profusely and hurt like hell. After cauterizing it with the smoke of a red-hot coal, Dude gazed into the crystal once more and determined that I was free of the harmful spirit energy.

---

2 Medicine men and shamans believe that all disease is caused by harmful spirits, called intrusions.

Dude Prepares a Crystal Medicine Healing

Later that evening, I brought my then partner to meet Dude, sure that he had also contracted an intrusion by virtue of his proximity to me. Sure enough, following a thorough coal and crystal search, Dude removed a small handful of anthill crystals from my partner's body via a painful incision made with the sharp edge of a flint.

Dude's crystal healing was very powerful medicine. While I have always been an advocate of the healing properties of crystals, gems, and minerals, the crystal doctoring I received from Dude soared above and beyond my wildest expectations of the healing power inherent in stones.

THE CRYSTAL HEALER

We have been given many natural tools to assist us in bringing about healing and wholeness: meditation, prayer, ritual, vitamins, herb, mineral, and nutritional therapies, massage, the laying on of hands, divination, and stones, to name just a few. However, an ancient axiom says: "The possession of Knowledge, unless accompanied by a manifestation and expression in Action, is like the hoarding of precious metals—a vain and foolish thing. Knowledge, like Wealth, is intended for Use. The Law of Use is Universal, and he who violates it suffers by reason of his conflict with natural forces."[3]

The Law of Use is a natural principle, a law of Nature. It maintains that in order to make knowledge, or anything else, our own, we must be able to employ it practically in everyday life—to use it to benefit ourselves and others, or lose it. Action clears the way for the unceasing flow of cosmic medicine, the Water of Life, to come into our lives. This open way of thinking and being—the ultimate prosperity consciousness—allows magical healing to take place on planet Earth as well as in the body-earth.

We cannot walk in beauty or be in harmony with the Earth Mother and her creation if we do not share what the cosmos has so freely given to us. A miserly response to this natural cosmic urge may have a devastating effect on the body, mind, and soul. When we refuse to share the abundance and prosperity we have received from the cosmos, however it may manifest in our lives, we create blockages in our ability to receive or transmit healing spirit energy. The electrons comprising our physical/auric bodies become close and dense, and light cannot flow in or out. This is when physical disease, emotional distress, mental imbalance, theft of spirit, and soul loss can occur.

Plains Indian medicine men use a preventative medicine procedure called Catch-the-Stone, which is similar to the yuwipi ceremony described in chapter 1. The Catch-the-Stone ceremony uses

---

3 Initiates, Three, *The Kybalion: Hermetic Philosophy* (Chicago, Yogi Publication Society), 1940, p. 213.

prayer, song, and spirit counseling, and provides the patient with a magic stone embodying a living spirit to protect against sickness and danger.[4] South American shamans will sometimes rub stones on the head and chest of a patient to prevent injury and disease. In medieval Europe, jacinth was the stone of choice in preserving the wearer against illness, especially the plague.[5]

We too may empower our lives by taking preventative measures to ensure good health, making sound use of the natural resources available to us, and helping ourselves and others to the extent that we are able. This last is all important, for as one very knowledgeable Brazilian shaman says: "We must first learn to love ourselves and other people before we are able to heal."

If you wish to be a healer, you must realize yourself as a channel of cosmic medicine, the Water of Life. Healing occurs because the spirit energy flowing in, through, and all around you is activated via divine intervention. You, the healer, do nothing but get out of the way so that the spirit energy may move freely in and through you.

Most tribal people do not take healing casually. Among the Sioux Indians there is usually much discussion by the patient with family, friends, and elders. Everything—the healer, the sickness or problem, and the proposed treatment—must be in harmony before the healer is sought to perform the work. Several more visits between the healer, the patient, and his or her family may be necessary before the healer accepts the job and the patient accepts the healer. Then the patient is required to follow certain preliminary actions before the actual healing takes place. These may include fasting, vision seeking, sweating, prayers, offerings, and giveaways or feasts, depending on tribal custom and the shaman or medicine person involved.[6]

As a healer, your goal is to earth the fiery, life-giving energies of the Great Spirit in the minds and bodies of those who come to you

---

4 Lewis, *The Medicine Men*, pp. 92–93.

5 Kunz, George Frederick, *The Curious Lore of Precious Stones* (New York, Dover Publications, Inc., 1971), p. 83.

6 Ibid, pp. 40–41.

for assistance. Your work takes you from the upper world of spirit to the lower world of soul, to change the perception as well as alter the rate of vibration in the mind and body of your patient, thus giving the person seeking a cure a glimpse into non-ordinary reality. When a person is temporarily removed from his or her present state of consciousness, these changes and alterations can bring about spontaneous healing.

Indigenous healers consider time an ally when it comes to the patient's ultimate recovery. They are aware that their very presence inspires hope and sets the patient's fears to rest. Therefore, one of the conditions necessary for a successful healing is *faith*. Faith forms a clairsentient link between you and your patient, enabling you to transmit vital spirit energy to the patient through the stones selected for healing. Establishing an open rapport with your patient at the onset of the healing enables you to work freely to bring about wholeness. Likewise, the patient should *expect* to achieve the desired state of wholeness. If the patient has doubts regarding you or your abilities, the results may be unstable.

However, you must never help a person who does not wish to be healed. This kind of behavior is a violation of natural law. One who insists on "helping" others against their will may simply be ignorant, or into dominance, manipulation, control, personal satisfaction, or gain. (Since you're reading these words, we can rule out ignorance as an excuse.)

The patient comes to you for treatment because he or she is out of alignment in some capacity, so you must be ready to compensate for his imbalance. You must see yourself as the spirit keeper of the people, as magical healing occurs because the healer talks to the spirits that live in stones (plants, animals, etc.) and receives an answer regarding the measures needed to produce wellness.

Following are several characteristics desirable in the balanced healing temperament. Ostensibly, a healer should be:

- Intelligent and efficient regarding patient care.

- Considerate, cheerful, and kind.

- Patient and firm.

- Courageous and imaginative.

- Objective, observant, and attentive.

- Healthy, strong, neat, clean, and orderly.

- Quiet and soft-spoken.

- Aware of the Otherworld and its effect on this world.

Healers usually have their own way of preparing the patient, for no two healers function exactly alike, and there are no hard and fast rules regarding technique. Above all the patient should be made to feel safe, secure, and relaxed, and to trust completely to your integrity, wisdom, and knowledge.

How you achieve a state of total relaxation in your patient depends on the problem requiring treatment. You may instruct the patient to sit, stand, or lie down. Restrictive clothing should be loosened or removed entirely and the patient offered a dressing gown of natural fabric and neutral color. I've heard of New Age and Wiccan healers and their patients working sky-clad (i.e. naked), but in my experience this is not necessary for successful results, nor have I ever witnessed contemporary tribal healers working in this manner.

Deep rhythmic breathing is important to total relaxation, as anxiety cannot exist where there is conscious breath. Therefore you may encourage and instruct your patient in this simple though potent preliminary therapy prior to the healing session. Several breaths taken deep into the abdomen through the nose and slowly exhaled through the mouth should suffice.

Balancing the System

You are likely to be confronted with many different types of problems in the healing work, which will fall into the categories of spiritual, mental, emotional, or physical disturbances, or a combination of some or all of these. However, even if the complaint is relegated to one specific area, you should set out to balance the entire system—body and mind, spirit and soul—in addition to treating the particular problem.

Here are some handy tips that you may use in preparation for the actual healing work:

If the problem is spiritual in nature, purify the atmosphere of your workspace with sage, cedar, or copal incense. The smoke from these herbs will soothe and calm your patient's aura.

Mental imbalances require some form of physical movement, such as yoga or stretching, prior to the healing session. The mental state is temporarily alleviated because the attention is focused on the body-earth.

Emotional difficulties respond well to sympathy and compassion. The emotionally distraught individual needs to feel safe and secure. You may achieve this by focusing on what your patient is feeling or experiencing, or by a brief period of gentle massage.

Once a problem manifests in the body-earth, it is harder to treat. In this case, you should ascertain that your patient has been diagnosed and treated by a licensed medical professional. This affords you protection against liability, and is helpful for determining the correct course of treatment.

As spirit energy collects in crystals, gems, and minerals, you may find yourself working with a variety of stones. Therefore, it is helpful to have many different stones on hand in order to work with them in a healing capacity. I like the method of letting the patient select the initial stones to be used for healing. This enables you to understand where the hidden or apparent deficiencies lie within the body-earth. Then you may select additional stones to treat the specific problem, if necessary. I have one or two stones that are my personal allies in healing work, as well as an odd assortment of stones constituting a backup team of healing helpers.

New Age crystal healers like Katrina Raphael, Jane Anne Dow, and Daya Sarai Chocron advocate the "laying on of stones" as a method of healing. I concur that this is an excellent process for auric cleansing and balancing the overall system. A method to employ the laying on of stones will be given in the following chapter. I also strongly advocate using shamanic methods for treatment, some of which I will share in chapter 7 also.

In addition, I recommend the use of sound, color, and strong mental images suggesting good health to transfer strength and power to the patient. Subtle suggestions stated over the course of the healing in the form of affirmations are also beneficial. Generally speaking, two or three resolute affirmations during the session are more effective than endless repetitive phrases.

When the healing session is complete, you may wish to assist your patient in closing down his or her aura, which has been opened up during treatment. A hot, soothing beverage, such as herbal tea, is an excellent way to close down the psychic centers. Certain stones, such as peridot, boji, or hematite, are excellent auric sealers. Have your patient hold one of these stones in the palm of the hand for approximately ten minutes before sending him or her on their way.

Sometimes it is necessary that your patient continue special treatment at home. If this is so, you may prescribe a method of self-healing, such as a particular crystal, gem, mineral, or metal, or a crystal tonic (see chapter 5).

Christine Le May

Choosing the Stone
Laying on of stones is an excellent process for auric
cleansing and balancing the overall system.

MEDICINE OFFERINGS AND GIVEAWAYS

The question often arises: should you solicit business to obtain patients, or charge a fee? Some healers rely on word of mouth, others on advertising in holistic health journals, etc. There are healers who refuse money, and others who charge an arm and a leg for their services.

A desperate person is often willing to pay anything to get free of his troubles. If you are sincere, you should be willing to help anyone who requests assistance, whether they can pay or not. A sliding fee scale or a suggested donation takes into account the patient's circumstances.

Among shamans, medicine people, and healers of many cultures and traditions, offerings and giveaways are a way to acknowledge medicine work. Keep the following ideas in mind when it is time for a show of gratitude, or make a copy to hand out to your prospective clients:

Smoke offerings clear the mind and cleanse the environment. The smoke carries prayers for the good of all creatures and things up to the Great Spirit, and to all directions. Dried cedar, sage, copal, and tobacco are among the most common herbs used for smoke offerings on this continent.

- Make a tobacco prayer tie: wrap loose-leaf, organic, or mountain tobacco in a square of 100% natural, red cotton cloth, and tie it up with a cotton string. A prayer tie that is offered to the Earth or to a medicine person or healer shows respect, gives the healer permission to pray for you, and shows that you are willing to be alert and use what you receive in a good way.

Green offerings are most helpful to the medicine person or healer who is working on you, because often he or she has mouths to feed and bills to pay, just like you. Green offerings may also be given to Mother Earth as a way of asking her for assistance and/or thanking her for the prosperity you enjoy on a daily basis. If you don't have green energy to give, please offer something useful, such as food or household items, or trade your special skills for the work being done.

- Make a green offering: fold U.S. currency around the outside of a tobacco prayer tie, and secure in place with suede or cotton string.

Fasting and sweat offerings can be used to purify the body, heart, and mind, or to relieve those who are suffering for whatever reason. Dancing, singing, and drumming fall into this category too.

- Make a fast or sweat offering: go without your favorite food or eat one less meal a day for a week, if possible; or partici-pate in a sweat lodge ceremony for someone less fortunate than you. Let the person know you are doing this for them.

Love offerings are always welcome by everyone. Start with bring-ing along a gracious, helpful attitude.

- Make a love offering: be part of the entire healing process.

Giveaways are celebrations. When you have received a healing, give gifts to those who have helped and shared in the experience with you.

- Make a giveaway: cook and serve a delicious feast with all the trimmings, or give personal treasures, such as stones you have collected; or create special things with certain individuals in mind.

DIVINING THE BODY-EARTH

Divination is a way of using our perception to predict past, present, or future events through a collaboration between our instincts, feelings, intellect, memory, and creative imagination. While hind-sight enables us to figure out how we have arrived at our present set of circumstances, and foresight gives us the ability to see events before they happen, our actions in the here and now are the most important, for these determine the extent to which we are open to guidance from the spirit world.

Some individuals are already attuned to the higher vibrational frequencies flowing in and through the Earth Mother at the present time. As the New Millennium approaches, we may all experience this acceleration of consciousness and perception, but even as we look to the sky for omens—sun spots, ozone depletion, and unusual planetary configurations—we must also look for changes in the Earth, including changes in the body-earth. Here on the planet is where it's all happening, or going to happen. Whatever is happening to the Earth is reflected in our physical body, and it is here in the body-earth that we must ultimately solve our problems.

Geomantic Divination

One ancient form of divination that enables us to recognize how the Earth is affected by the cosmos is geomancy. This system employs spirit energy (electromagnetism) to ascertain the meaning of changes and patterns in the Earth. Dowsing, the method used in geomantic divination, assists us in determining which way the flow is going so that we can flow with it, if this is what we choose.

The practice of dowsing for ley lines, the energy patterns in the Earth, sometimes uses figures or lines formed by a handful of dirt cast on the ground. Tibetan and Navajo healers draw sand-paintings in the course of their healing ceremonies. The Oglala Sioux Catch-the-Stone ceremony uses a bucket of dirt gathered from gopher hills. This earth is smoothed out on the floor for the altar and on it the medicine person draws dots and furrows with his finger.[7]

In dowsing, a forked stick called a divining rod is employed to attract the electromagnetic currents that live in the ground. In water witching, the point of the forked dowsing rod is drawn downward toward the ground when the water source is located. Oil, lost objects, missing persons, buried treasure, and precious gems may be found by dowsing in this way, or a pendulum, an object suspended from a fixed point so as to swing freely to and fro, is often used as well. The pendulum will begin swinging or change directions when the desired object is located.

---

7 Lewis, *The Medicine Men*, p. 91.

Dowsing with a pendulum can help us to ascertain the condition of the body, mind, and spirit. This ancient method of dowsing the body is in modern times known as radionics or radiesthesia. The old and new versions of this system are the same, as both use perception to detect the vibrations, force fields, or heat rays emanating from the person, place, or thing being dowsed. Cosmic or electro-magnetic energies are the force fields in the aura radiating from the body-earth. Dowsing assists us in contacting these energy fields and measuring them.

How is this done? First, it is important to get in touch with the water within the body in order to dowse properly. Water is known to conduct energy currents, such as electricity, in order to produce heat and light. This element comes in many forms: streams, rivers, lakes, and oceans, falling from the clouds as rain, or in body fluids and secretions, such as urine, saliva, tears, gastric and pancreatic juices, the amniotic fluid surrounding the fetus during pregnancy, and the blood. Human emotion is the metaphoric water of the body.

Underground veins of water produce places on the Earth's surface where female and male energies meet to form power spots. Spider Rock in Chinle, Arizona, the Red Rocks in Sedona, or Stonehenge and Avebury in England, are all examples of sacred power spots. I recall the strong scent of sea-salted air while visiting Stonehenge, although there was no ocean within thirty-five miles. I later discovered that the entire Salisbury Plain, where Stonehenge was erected, was once under water.

MERIDIANS AND THE FLOW OF ENERGY

The energies gathered at power spots shift with the seasons, each place reaching its peak of power at various times throughout the year, depending on the course of the planets and stars. The spirit energy centers in the aura surrounding the body-earth respond in much the same manner as the power centers scattered over the Earth. The male and female currents of the body-earth meet at various points located in the endocrine system, where the glands

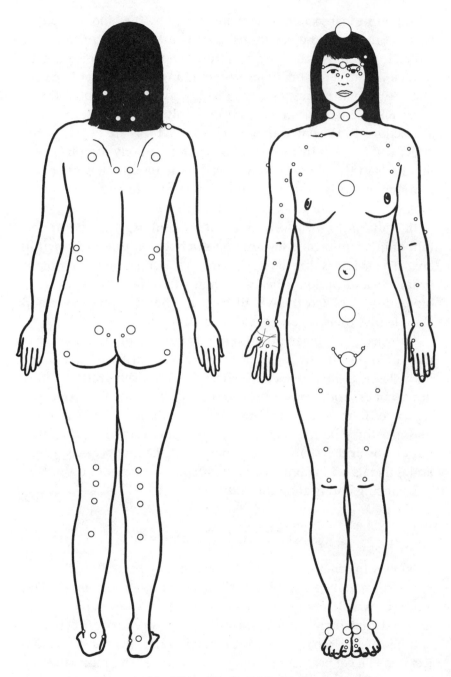

Meridians on the Body-Earth

produce internal secretions that are carried by the blood or lymph to the organs whose functions they regulate and control. The endocrine glands—the pineal, pituitary, thyroid, and adrenals located in the central nervous system along with the cardiac ganglion, the solar plexus, and the sacral plexus (see chapter 4: The Seven Spirit Energy Centers)—are all highly sensitive to our visceral reactions to the environment. If our reactions are negative, the effect will be seen in the astral or emotional body long before it manifests in the physical body. Because the natural flow of energy in these centers is so easily disrupted, they should be dowsed when looking for holes or weak spots in the aura.

In addition to the seven spirit energy centers, there are important points comprising ley lines on the body-earth, called meridians. The vital spirit energy running along these meridians promotes and prolongs health. When the flow of vital energy is blocked or depleted there is ill health; when it flows freely and abundantly, there is good health and well-being.

Knowledge of the anatomical points connecting the meridians may be used effectively to detect potential disharmony in the body. These points are located where the flesh, veins, arteries, tendons, bones, and joints meet together (as illustrated on page 97). Injury to these points can cause severe disability, even death. Via massage, these points may be used to stimulate and heal the internal organs and systems of the body-earth. Laying crystals, gems, and minerals on the points and meridians is another effective way of balancing and healing the body-earth.

CRYSTAL DOWSING

The following method of crystal dowsing may be used to discern a predilection to illness in the body. This method can be performed on a subject, whether or not he or she is present. However, please keep in mind that permission is essential when working on behalf of another, even if what you do is to their ultimate benefit. If the subject is too ill, get permission from a close relative. This forms an emotional link between the dowser and the subject. Also, keep your ego in check. Believe in your own power, but know that the Great Spirit does the actual work. If you believe that you are doing the actual healing, you will eventually deplete your life force and place your own health in jeopardy. Remember, you are the transmitter of spirit energy, not the source. Finally, once you have ascertained the problem, and especially if it appears to be serious, get a sound diagnosis from a certified medical practitioner before rendering treatment.

To Dowse

Obtain a pendulum. This can be any object hanging from a string, from an old house key dangling from a piece of dental floss to a crystal suspended from a silken cord. I use a dainty, clear quartz crystal point inset with peridot, bound with silver, and hung on a fine silver chain. A friend of mine used a hefty clear quartz record-keeper (see record keeper discussion on page 182) dangling from a soft, deerhide thong.[8]

Draw an outline of a body and below it write the name of the person you intend to dowse. This will help you to focus your attention on the person you are dowsing.

Think about what you are about to do. Pray to the powers that be for assistance and guidance.

When you feel ready, hold your pendulum in the search position, suspended between the thumb and index finger of your left hand (reverse this position if you are left-handed). Begin dowsing by running the pendulum down the figure you have drawn, starting at the top of the head. When you come to a problem, the pendulum will begin to move from a stationary position to form some other pattern, as follows:

- Forth and back (male and female, electric and magnetic).

- Clockwise (male, electric).

- Counter-clockwise (female, magnetic).

---

8   The crystal from my friend's pendulum literally jumped from the Chevy Blazer during a 1996 roadtrip through the Pacific Northwest. We suppose it's somewhere in what remains of the wooded outskirts of Roslyn, Washington, where the TV series *Northern Exposure* was filmed.

These directions will let you know if the energy you are dealing with is aggressive (male, electric) or passive (female, magnetic), as well as where in the body the potential problem is located. Usually, clockwise means "yes," and counter-clockwise means "no"; however, this is not always the case. For example, my pendulum is a totally contrary spirit, so it is better to ask the spirit in the crystal pendulum which way is "yes" at the onset.

Use of the crystal pendulum will increase your ability to prevent disease or assist in bringing about healing through preventative measures, should the problem be apparent.

In order to select the appropriate crystal medicine, you may also dowse stones and elixirs that fall into the applicable category for the problem being treated. Many of these stones may be found in the crystal encyclopedia in chapter 8.

THE MEDICINE WHEEL

Before we begin to work with stones for healing, we must center ourselves in relation to the Earth and the creatures and things living on her turtle back, or, as Hyemeyohsts Storm says, "Let us teach each other here in this Great Lodge of the People, this Sun Dance, of each of the Ways on this Great Medicine Wheel, our Earth."[9]

The simplest Medicine Wheel is constructed of many stones, large and small. Each stone represents you and me, our families and friends, the four-leggeds, wingeds and creepy-crawlies, the standing people and the stone people, as well as governments, religions, and philosophies.

The four great powers on the Medicine Wheel begin in the north, the place of wisdom. It is colored white and its power animal is Buffalo. The south is the place of innocence. Its color is red and its power animal is Mouse. Introspection is attributed to the west. Its color is black and its power animal is Bear. East is the place of enlightenment. Its color is yellow and its power animal is Eagle.[10] Winter may be associated with the north, summer with the

9 Storm, Hyemeyohsts, *Seven Arrows* (New York, Ballentine Books, 1972), p. 1.

10 Note that the four colors of the Medicine Wheel are synonymous with the four alchemical colors listed in chapter 5.

south, spring with the east, and fall with the west. In addition to the four directions, white, red, black, and yellow represent to the Lakota Indians the four seasons, the four periods of life and aging, and the four races of humanity. When mixed together, the resulting color is brown, the color of the fifth race—a unified people.[11]

The gathering together of many creatures and things within the circle of the wheel symbolizes the harmony shared by all. We must learn to look at life from the perspective of each of the four great powers in order to become a whole person.[12]

A Medicine Wheel
This simple wheel will give an earth connection to your healing rituals.

11 Means, Russel, with Wolf, Marvin J., *Where White Men Fear to Tread: The Autobiography of Russel Means* (New York, St. Martin's Press, 1995), p. 553.
12 Elsbeth, Marguerite, "The Medicine Wheel," *Llewellyn's 1996 Magical Almanac*

⇥ CRYSTAL MEDICINE 6 ⇤
HOW TO MAKE A MEDICINE WHEEL

First, gather one large stone, twenty medium stones, and twelve smaller stones—thirty-three stones in all.

1. Designate an area for your circle, preferably out of doors. The circle should be big enough for you to stand comfortably at each of the four directions.

2. Place the largest stone in the center of the circle to represent the Earth. Then position seven medium stones around the center stone in acknowledgment of each of the elemental clans—Fire, Water, Air, Earth, the Earth Mother, Grandmother Moon, and Father Sun.[13] Next, choose four more medium-sized stones. These are called spirit keepers and are to be placed at the four directions of the outside diameter of the circle, east, west, north, and south. Move counterclockwise, starting with north at the top, followed by west, south, and east.

3. Twelve more medium stones comprise the twelve moons of the Medicine Wheel, the sacred shields.[14] Place three of these stones between each of the four directions.

4. Finally, stone pathways are positioned between the four quarters of the wheel—spokes that extend outward from the inner circle of seven stones to each of the four spirit keepers. Fill in these pathways with the rest of the stones.

You are now ready to begin your journey around the wheel of life.[15]

---

13 The seven stones may also be associated with the seven colors of the rainbow, the seven ancient planets, and the seven spirit energy centers.

14 The twelve small stones may also be associated with the twelve constellations or astrological signs.

15 *Llewellyn's 1996 Magical Almanac*, pp. 52–53.

To Use the Medicine Wheel:

1. Designate an area for your circle, preferably out of doors. Burn sage or cedar herbs. Smudge yourself and the Medicine Wheel. This is done by placing the sage in a shell, lighting it afire, and offering it to the six directions. Facing east, take a feather, hold the sage up, and fan the smoke to Sky Father above; lower the sage and fan the smoke to Earth Mother below. Next, extend the sage before you and smudge the east; then turn to face and smudge the west. Turn to smudge the north and turn to smudge the south. Remember to pray in your own way, asking for the things you want, and offering gratitude for what you already have. Face east again and use the feather to move the smoke over your body, from the bottom of your feet (earth) up to your head (sky). Pray for purity of heart and mind as the smoke passes over your chest and head. Say a prayer to the Great Spirit, asking for illumination and guidance.[16]

2. Now, again facing the east, call upon Eagle to take your prayers to the Great Spirit. Receive a blessing from the east. Turn toward the south and ask Mouse for innocence. Feel the blessing of the south. Face the west and ask Bear to give you strength and courage. Accept the blessing of the west. Turn and face north. Call upon Buffalo to give you the wisdom to apply all that you have learned from Eagle, Mouse, and Bear. Receive the blessing of the north.

3. Finally, look at the Earth, the stone in the center of the circle. Touch it and feel the protection the Great Spirit and the Earth Mother offer you. Again, face the four directions in turn, giving thanks to the spirit keepers, the stones, for the help you have received. Take a few moments to think about what you have experienced.[17]

---

16 Ibid, pp. 110–111.
17 Ibid, pp. 52–53.

CHAPTER 6

Once you have built a Medicine Wheel and consecrated it as outlined, you may use it for dowsing and/or treating people in your healing work.

7

MORE CRYSTAL MEDICINES

REMEDIES
Being Earth-centered demands that we "walk our talk"; therefore, this chapter embodies more of the practical work of healing with stones. The following medicines include shamanic and alchemical techniques that have been used successfully by practicing healers from various cultures all over the world. With a little practice, these remedies will work for you also.

CHAPTER 7

⇥ CRYSTAL MEDICINE 7 ⇤
CRYSTAL CLEARING

When you first acquire a stone, it is a good idea to clear it of all previous vibrations before putting it to use, because you don't know where it's been, or what psychic impressions it has absorbed during the course of its travels. Following are several known methods of crystal clearing:

Sea Salt Clearing

To clear a crystal, gem, or mineral with sea salt, you will need:
   1 cup of purified water
   1/8 cup of sea salt
   A glass or bowl

   Place the water in the glass. Add sea salt. Put your stone in the water and sea salt solution. Let it stand overnight, or dowse the water with your pendulum to see if the stone is clear. This can be determined with a "yes" or "no" answer.

Earth Clearing

To clear a crystal, gem, or mineral with earth, find a secluded place out of doors. Dig until you reach a point where the earth is fresh, usually about six inches down. Plant the stone in the hole, and cover it up with dirt. Mark the spot with a large rock. (If you have constructed the Medicine Wheel outlined in the previous chapter, bury the stone under the large rock in the center of the wheel.) If you don't have access to the outdoors, bury the stone in a flower pot. Keep the stone buried overnight, or dowse the spot with your pendulum to determine if the stone is clear and ready to come out.

Sun Clearing

To clear a stone with sunlight, first make sure it is colorfast (usually, colored quartz crystals such as citrine and amethyst fade in the sun). Then, simply wait for a sunny day and place the stone outside for several hours. Dowse the stone to see if it has soaked up enough rays. (See page 95 for dowsing methods.)

Natural Water Clearing

Go to the shallow bank of a river or stream. Place the stone to be cleared in a fine mesh pouch (I usually cut the foot off a nylon stocking). Secure the pouch so it doesn't wash away in the water, and leave it overnight.

Smudge Clearing

To smudge clear a stone, place sage, cedar, or copal herbs in a shell or heat-proof container. Facing east, light the herbs and offer the smoke to the six directions, as outlined in "The Medicine Wheel" section in chapter 6. (If you have constructed a Medicine Wheel, perform this ceremony within the circle, using the central stone as your altar or table.) Have the stone to be smudged ready in front of you. When the blessing of the directions is complete fan the smoke over the stone, or hold the stone in the smoke. Pray to the Great Spirit in your own way, asking that the stone be clear of all harmful vibrations.

Christine Le May

Smudge Clearing a Stone

109

ᐸ CRYSTAL MEDICINE 8 ᐳ
CRYSTAL EMPOWERMENT

Crystals, gems, and minerals may be charged with energy to serve a specific purpose. This medicine lends power to the stone, and tells the spirit in the stone what you expect of it. Stones may be charged for a variety of reasons—vitality, love, good health, prosperity, creativity, etc. However, in my experience, it is always best to first ask the stone spirit what it may be used for and proceed from there, rather than tell it what to do. If this doesn't work for you, use your intuition or refer to the properties listed in the crystal encyclopedia in chapter 8 to see how you may best work with a particular stone. Also, see the section titled "The Planets" in chapter 1, or "The Seven Spirit Energy Centers" in chapter 4, for further information regarding luminary and planetary energies.

Sun Power

Use this medicine to charge a stone with electricity, creativity, vitality, purpose, and authority. To charge a stone with sun power, you will need:

A stone
1 cup of purified water
A glass or bowl
A sunny day

Put the water and the stone in the glass or bowl. Place the container outside in the sun or on a sunny window sill indoors for several hours. Dowse the stone to see if it is charged.

Moon Power

Use this medicine to charge a stone with magnetism, intuition, memories, and emotions. To charge a stone with moon power, you will need:

A stone
1 cup of purified water
A glass or bowl
A waxing moon

Put the water and the stone in the glass or bowl. Place it out of doors under the moonlight or on a moonlit window sill indoors for several hours. Dowse the stone to see if it is charged.

Planet Power

Crystals, gems, and minerals may be charged with the energies of the planets. To charge a stone with planetary power, first refer to an ephemeris or almanac to determine the correct planetary position for your purpose. Then, see the section titled "The Planets" in chapter 1, or "The Seven Spirit Energy Centers" in chapter 4, for further information. Proceed as outlined in the Sun and Moon Power medicines, using sunlight for the Sun, Mercury, Mars, Jupiter, and Uranus, and moonlight for the Moon, Venus, Saturn, Neptune, and Pluto.

Star Power

Crystals, gems, and minerals may be charged with the energies of the constellations. To charge a stone with star power, refer to an ephemeris or almanac to determine the predominant constellations that the sun, moon, and planets occupy. Then, see the section titled "The Planets" in chapter 1, or "The Seven Spirit Energy Centers" in chapter 4, for further information. Proceed as outlined in the Sun and Moon Power medicines, using sunlight for Aries, Gemini, Leo, Libra, Sagittarius, and Aquarius, and moonlight for Taurus, Cancer, Virgo, Scorpio, Capricorn, and Pisces.

Elemental Power

To charge stones with the power of the elements, proceed as suggested in Crystal Medicine 8 in chapter 6. Fire and Air are fundamental properties of the Sun, while Water and Earth may be associated with the Moon.

The Power of Intent

Hold the stone to be charged in the closed palm of whichever hand you feel is more receptive. Ask the stone spirit for permission to charge it with a specific purpose. Concentrate your purpose into the stone. Thank the stone spirit.

Shamanic Crystal Medicines

The shaman's magic is produced through a combination of strong personal will, imagination, and a happy relationship with Mother Earth. He or she also adheres to the fundamental belief that all creatures and things, animate and inanimate, contain a living spirit. This belief is the true source of all shamanic magic and power. It is from this viewpoint that the shaman works with stones.

Christine Le May

Empowering a Crystal
It is best to first ask the stone spirit what it may be used for and proceed from there, rather than tell it what to do.

⇒ CRYSTAL MEDICINE 9 ⇐
THE STONE OF LIGHT

The phrase "stone of light" comes from the Mayan word *sastun*. A sastun is a seeing stone used to divine problems relating to the mind, body, or soul. This stone comes as a gift to the shaman. Much to the shaman's surprise, the stone of light is often received through a strange set of circumstances; it can fall from the sky and land at one's feet! (Remember Holy Dance from the previous chapter, and how he found his healing stones.) Sometimes the stone is already in the shaman's possession; he or she just doesn't know it yet.

A stone of light embodies unusual powers and can take many forms. It can be any transparent stone at all: a quartz crystal or a colorful child's marble. The diviner should be able to see the light of the stone sparkle and shine when the stone is moved, and the interior should have some distinguishing marks or pictures, such as dots, crosses, lines, a landscape, angels, rainbows, clouds, or animals. The diviner should have a gift to see inside the stone.

Some stones have a variety of uses, and other stones can be used only for one purpose: to see if a person in need of healing can be cured, for example.

The seeing stone demands much attention. First, determine if you already have one. If you don't, pray for one and it may come to you when you least expect it.

Knowing the Stone of Light

1. Take a clear stone or crystal that stands above all the other stones in your keeping.

2. Blow on it three times and place it in the palm of your hand. Blow on it three more times, put it into a pouch or other container (see below), and swirl it around while praying to the Great Spirit for help and guidance. Repeat the words "stone of light" several times, along with your name.

3. Hold the stone in the palm of your hand again, and ask the spirits for a dream that will tell you how to use it, read it,

113

and care for it. Be aware of the spirits that visit you in your dreams and carefully follow their directions regarding your stone of light.

Empowering Your Stone of Light

You and the spirits have determined that your crystal is a seeing stone.

1. Now gaze into it and call to the spirit of the stone of light. Ask for wisdom, dreams, and answers.

2. As you are doing so, make the sign of the equal-armed cross (+) on both sides of the crystal, dipping your finger in rum each time. (Alcohol is used to bathe the stone due to its antibacterial properties, using the reasoning that if it's good enough for snake bite, it will also chase evil spirits away while propitiating the good ones. Rum is used in South America because it is most inexpensive to obtain, but actually any hard liquor will do.)

3. Do this nine times in a row, every Friday, for the rest of your life.

Cleaning Your Stone of Light

Once you have begun to work with your stone, bathe it in rum once a week to clear it of questions and old vibrations.

Storing Your Stone of Light

Finally, keep the stone of light in a beautiful leather pouch, an old fruit jar, on a cord around your neck, or wherever else you have perceived the spirits want you to keep it.[1]

---

1 Elsbeth, Marguerite, *Llewellyn's 1996 Magical Almanac*, "The Shaman's Sastun," p. 96–97. In this article I have given suggestions for ways to store these stones.

⇥ CRYSTAL MEDICINE 10 ⇤
CRYSTAL COAL DIVINATION

Shamans often use a clear quartz crystal for the purpose of divination. Crystal and coal combine the elements of Fire and Earth. When divining with crystal and coal, we ask these elements to help us solve our problems. The following medicine is similar to the Navajo divination method described in chapter 6.

You will need:
Sage, cedar, or copal herbs
An old baking pan
Self-starting coals
A small shovel or tongs
A medium to large clear quartz crystal point,
    or a stone of light

1. Heat the coals in the baking pan until they are red-hot and glowing. Remove your stone of light (or your favorite crystal) from its special pouch and place it in front of you.

2. Sprinkle the sage, cedar, or copal on the coals, all the time praying to the Great Spirit for help. Use your own words to talk to the Creator. Say whatever is on your mind and in your heart.

3. Now, hold the crystal between your thumb and forefinger, in the hand that feels most receptive. Gaze through the crystal at the glowing coal embers. What do you see? What do you feel? Go with the thoughts, feelings, and images that spontaneously arise before you. Your first impressions are usually the correct ones for assessing the situation.

4. Follow your instincts and proceed with healing the condition through whatever method seems right to you.

CHAPTER 7

NEW AGE CRYSTAL MEDICINE

Followers of New Age thought have been most instrumental in bringing the healing energies of stones to our attention. Since the late 1980s, New Age use of crystals, gems, and minerals has evolved from simple meditative techniques and jewelry to psi-tech implements such as Atlantean power rods and psionic beam generators, called autoelectromags (AEM).[2]

Some New Age crystal healers claim to share close contact with the Pleiades. Others believe that their ability to work with stones comes from past-life memories associated with Atlantis and Lemuria, or that the information they receive regarding stones is channeled through spirit guides, animal totems, the deceased, angels, or other highly evolved beings of light. Then there are certain so-called New Age healers, spiritual voyeurs who flit from path to path, listing all of the above phenomena as the root source of their power.

Sometimes it seems that for the New Age crystal healer, the more phantasmagoric the power source, the better. However, the power sources cited by most New Age healers bear a striking resemblance to those used by shamans and medicine people all over the world. Otherworldly visitors, spirits, animals, and the ancestors all play an important role in the magical intercession engendered by indigenous healers. The difference may be that some New Age healers mistake these entities (or even themselves) for the source of healing power, while shamans and medicine people realize them as helpers and guides only, not the actual source of power.

Actually, shamans and medicine people work from the same land base in the same community for many years. They don't attain their status as healers overnight. A lifetime of training in stones, herbs, emotions, and spiritual belief is required—their knowledge doesn't just drop out of the cosmos. They need to have the wisdom to send a person to another doctor when the person can't be healed with stones and prayer alone, because they know

---

2 Smith, Michael G., and Lin Westhorp, *Crystal Warrior: Shamanic Transformation & Projection of Universal Energy* (St. Paul: Llewellyn Publications, 1992), p. 19.

that most of the time it takes a combination of methods to effect a cure.

Indigenous healers realize that the real healing power source is far more ancient (the New Age notwithstanding), a universal energy animating, vivifying, and ensouling all that inhabits human perceptual awareness. Whether we refer to it as electromagnetism, spiritual ether, limitless light, *prana* or *prakriti*, Great Spirit, Great Mystery, or spirit energy, this universal power is both the healer and the medicine. We do nothing, and everything else—the space aliens, the spirits, the critters, the dead relatives, and the light beings—are friends and allies we may trust for guidance, if we choose. But it's not really necessary.

Whatever the supposed or imagined source of New Age crystal healing power, I have found the New Age technique of laying on of stones to be quite effective to enhance meditation and auric balancing, as well as for directing and projecting healing energy throughout the body-earth.[3]

---

3 Please refer to Katrina Raphael's *Crystal Enlightenment: The Transforming Properties of Crystals and Healing Stones*, Vol. 1 (New York, Aurora Press. 1986) or *Healing with Crystals and Gemstones* (York Beach, ME: Samuel Weiser, Inc., 1986) by Daya Sarai Chocron, for more extensive information regarding the various techniques of the laying on of stones.

⫷ CRYSTAL MEDICINE 11 ⫸
THE LAYING ON OF STONES

The laying on of stones requires that you have a large stock of crystals, gems, and minerals at hand. To begin, have the person who is to receive treatment select stones to which he or she feels attracted. Use these stones as well as any others you think may be helpful to bring about wholeness and balance.

Have the person loosen any restrictive clothing and lie down on the earth, the floor, a bed, or a massage table. Encourage him or her to breathe deeply until he or she feels relaxed. Meanwhile, do whatever is necessary to center yourself.

The stones may be placed on the spirit energy centers of the body, or on any area that seems to be unbalanced, congested, or uncomfortable. Be spontaneous and allow your intuition to guide you in the moment. The various patterns created on the body with the stones will direct the flow of energy where it needs to go.

Christine Le May

Stone Healing
The author conducts a healing by the laying on of stones.

Once you have arranged all the stones in place, allow them to remain on the body for as long as seems necessary. However, remove the stones immediately if the person you are treating experiences discomfort such as numbness in the limbs, headaches, dizziness, or emotional distress.

When the treatment is complete, have the person lie quietly for several minutes before rising. End the session with a sense of gratitude, a hot herbal beverage, and a light snack.

Alchemical Crystal Medicine

Sound is the rhythm of the universe and the cosmic Water of Life. The first alchemist used sound in the form of incantation to bring about desired changes in the vibratory sphere of the body-earth. Every sound produces a certain color and form. Likewise, stones emit healing sound vibrations. The use of compatible sounds, colors, and stones produces powerful results, as this combination of energies works to alter the electronic composition of the body-earth and its surrounding auric field, thus preventing or eliminating disease.

Should you decide to try the following medicines, please be thorough and make haste slowly.

⇥ CRYSTAL MEDICINE 12 ⇤
CRYSTAL INCANTATION

Crystal incantation is a method derived from the Western occult tradition, such as Israel Regardie's use of colors and god-name vibration on the chakras in his work titled *The Art of True Healing*.

To heal what ails you or others through crystal incantation, you will eventually wish to gather a wide variety of metals and stones. A pitch pipe will help you to register perfect tones throughout the physical and auric bodies. However, the actual incantation is produced with the sacred sound of your own voice. You may make any sound you wish, a low, guttural cry or the cosmic OM; however, the intonation should reverberate throughout the head, throat, and chest areas if it is to produce the desired results.

As with all spiritual work, it is important to approach incantation medicine with reverence. Remember never to concentrate energy directly on the spirit energy centers, as this could result in further emotional, mental, or physical imbalance. The use of sound, color, and the appropriate stones automatically initiates stimulation of the centers to promote healing.

Also, please note that although I've indicated the use of specific colors and minerals in association with the seven spirit energy centers and twelve body areas that follow, you may use any colors or stones that feel natural or "right" to you.

Singing the Spirit Energy Centers

When working to heal a specific problem for yourself or others, you must first prepare and awaken the spirit energy centers. To begin:

1. Review the physical, emotional, and mental attributes of the spirit energy centers outlined in chapter 4.

2. Sit comfortably. Have your pitch pipe handy, and the stones corresponding to the seven centers in front of you, as follows:

   Saturn = Galena
   Mars = Hematite or Carnelian

Jupiter = Tin
Sun = Gold
Venus = Copper
Moon = Silver
Mercury = Quicksilver or Cinnabar ☿ (in the proper container)

3. Take several deep breaths to relax, or do Crystal Medicine 1: Drawing Energy from the Earth, as outlined in chapter 1.

You are now ready to awaken the seven spirit energy centers.

Saturn

1. Pick up the galena crystal and hold it in the palm of your receptive hand.

2. Close your eyes and visualize vibrant, blue-black, indigo light surrounding you and filling every fiber of your being.

3. Sound the note A Natural on the pitch pipe. Hold the indigo color in and around you as you sing the note after sounding it. Make the effort, even if you encounter difficulty, for it is your intention that matters.

Mars

1. Pick up the hematite or carnelian crystal and hold it in the palm of your receptive hand.

2. Close your eyes and visualize vibrant red light surrounding you and filling every fiber of your being.

3. Sound the note C Natural on the pitch pipe. Hold the red color as you sing the note after sounding it.

Jupiter

1. Pick up the tin and hold it in the palm of your receptive hand.

2. Close your eyes and visualize vibrant violet light surrounding you and filling every fiber of your being.

3. Sound the note A Natural on the pitch pipe. Hold the violet color as you sing the note after sounding it.

Sun

1. Pick up the gold and hold it in the palm of your receptive hand.

2. Close your eyes and visualize vibrant orange light surrounding you and filling every fiber of your being.

3. Sound the note D Natural on the pitch pipe. Hold the orange color as you sing the note after sounding it.

Venus

1. Pick up the copper and hold it in the palm of your receptive hand.

2. Close your eyes and visualize vibrant green light surrounding you and filling every fiber of your being.

3. Sound the note F Sharp on the pitch pipe. Hold the green color as you sing the note after sounding it.

Moon

1. Pick up the silver and hold it in the palm of your receptive hand.

2. Close your eyes and visualize vibrant blue light surrounding you and filling every fiber of your being.

3. Sound the note G Sharp on the pitch pipe. Hold the blue color as you sing the note after sounding it.

Mercury

1. Pick up the quicksilver ☿ (**in a glass container, please— highly toxic, use with great caution**) or cinnabar crystal and hold it in the palm of your receptive hand.

2. Close your eyes and visualize vibrant yellow light surrounding you and filling every fiber of your being.

3. Sound the note E Natural on the pitch pipe. Hold the yellow color as you sing the note after sounding it.

Singing the Body-Earth

Now you are ready to balance and awaken the twelve areas of the body-earth. Have the stones corresponding to the twelve bodily areas ready in front of you, as follows:

Aries = Rutile, Cassiterite, Apophyllite, or Zircon
Taurus = Marcasite, Chrysoberyl, Olivine, or Topaz
Gemini = Diamond, Pyrite, Fluorite, Sodalite, Garnet, or Lapis
   Lazuli
Cancer = Quartz, Jasper, or Agate
Leo = Sulphur, Marcasite, Chrysoberyl, Peridot, or Topaz
Virgo = Dioptase, Calcite, Apatite, Beryl, Tourmaline,
   Corundum, Citrine, or Smoky Quartz
Libra = Turquoise or Wulfenite
Scorpio = Marcasite, Chrysoberyl, Olivine, or Topaz
Sagittarius = Amethyst, Chalcedony, or Fire Opal
Capricorn = Rutile, Cassiterite, Apophyllite, or Zircon
Aquarius = Diamond, Pyrite, Fluorite, Sodalite, or Lapis Lazuli
Pisces = Malachite, Azurite, Selenite, Serpentine,
   Diopside, Neptunite, Chrysocholla, or Jadeite

Aries

1. Pick up the stone for Aries and hold it in the palm of your receptive hand.

2. Close your eyes and visualize vibrant red light surrounding you and filling every fiber of your being.

3. Sound the note C Natural on the pitch pipe. Hold the red color as you sing the note after sounding it.

Taurus

1. Pick up the stone for Taurus and hold it in the palm of your receptive hand.

2. Close your eyes and visualize vibrant red-orange light surrounding you and filling every fiber of your being.

3. Sound the note C Sharp on the pitch pipe. Hold the red-orange color as you sing the note after sounding it.

Gemini

1. Pick up the stone for Gemini and hold it in the palm of your receptive hand.

2. Close your eyes and visualize vibrant orange light surrounding you and filling every fiber of your being.

3. Sound the note D Natural on the pitch pipe. Hold the orange color as you sing the note after sounding it.

Cancer

1. Pick up the stone for Cancer and hold it in the palm of your receptive hand.

2. Close your eyes and visualize vibrant orange-yellow light surrounding you and filling every fiber of your being.

3. Sound the note D Sharp on the pitch pipe. Hold the orange-yellow color as you sing the note after sounding it.

Leo

1. Pick up the stone for Leo and hold it in the palm of your receptive hand.

2. Close your eyes and visualize vibrant yellow light surrounding you and filling every fiber of your being.

3. Sound the note E Natural on the pitch pipe. Hold the yellow color as you sing the note after sounding it.

Virgo

1. Pick up the stone for Virgo and hold it in the palm of your receptive hand.

2. Close your eyes and visualize vibrant yellow-green light surrounding you and filling every fiber of your being.

3. Sound the note F Natural on the pitch pipe. Hold the yellow-green color as you sing the note after sounding it.

Libra

1. Pick up the stone for Libra and hold it in the palm of your receptive hand.

2. Close your eyes and visualize vibrant green light surrounding you and filling every fiber of your being.

3. Sound the note F Sharp on the pitch pipe. Hold the green color as you sing the note after sounding it.

Scorpio

1. Pick up the stone for Scorpio and hold it in the palm of your receptive hand.

2. Close your eyes and visualize vibrant red light surrounding you and filling every fiber of your being.

3. Sound the note G Natural on the pitch pipe. Hold the red color as you sing the note after sounding it.

Sagittarius

1. Pick up the stone for Sagittarius and hold it in the palm of your receptive hand.

2. Close your eyes and visualize vibrant blue light surrounding you and filling every fiber of your being.

3. Sound the note G Sharp on the pitch pipe. Hold the blue color as you sing the note after sounding it.

Capricorn

1. Pick up the stone for Capricorn and hold it in the palm of your receptive hand.

2. Close your eyes and visualize vibrant indigo light surrounding you and filling every fiber of your being.

3. Sound the note A Natural on the pitch pipe. Hold the indigo color as you sing the note after sounding it.

Aquarius

1. Pick up the stone for Aquarius and hold it in the palm of your receptive hand.

2. Close your eyes and visualize vibrant violet light surrounding you and filling every fiber of your being.

3. Sound the note A Sharp on the pitch pipe. Hold the violet color as you sing the note after sounding it.

Pisces

1. Pick up the stone for Pisces and hold it in the palm of your receptive hand.

2. Close your eyes and visualize vibrant violet-red light surrounding you and filling every fiber of your being.

3. Sound the note B Natural on the pitch pipe. Hold the violet-red color as you sing the note after sounding it.

⇥ CRYSTAL MEDICINE 13 ⇤
SONGS FOR SPECIFIC PROBLEMS

Now that you have completed the medicines for awakening the seven spirit energy centers and the twelve body areas, you may proceed with the following medicines for healing specifically diseased or problematic areas.

Remember, when treating inflammatory conditions, begin with a warm color and end with its color complement. The color complements are:

Red and Green
Red-Orange and Blue-Green
Orange and Blue
Yellow-Orange and Blue-Violet
Yellow and Violet
Yellow-Green and Violet-Red

1. First, refer to the following Reference List for Alchemical Crystal Healing to find the specific problem. For example, a headache would be treated with red, an Aries stone, and C Natural, followed by green, a Libra stone, and F Sharp as follows:

2. Have the Aries stone and the Libra stone in front of you.

3. Hold the Aries stone in the palm of your receptive hand.

4. Close your eyes, and surround and fill the head area with vibrant red color while singing the note C Natural (use the pitch pipe if necessary).

5. Now, imagine the red light turning a vivid, healthy green.

6. Put down the Aries stone and hold the Libra stone in the palm of your receptive hand.

7. Surround and fill the head area with vibrant green color while singing the note F Sharp.

8. If pain is present, always finish up with the color blue, silver, and G Sharp.

127

CHAPTER 7

REFERENCE LIST FOR
ALCHEMICAL CRYSTAL HEALING

Symptom	Color	Note	Stones
Abdomen	Yellow-Green	F	Virgo
	Red-Violet	B	Pisces
Adenoids	Blue-Green	G	Scorpio
AIDS	Red	C	Mars/Aries
	Yellow	E	Mercury/Leo
	Orange	D	Sun/Gemini
Alcoholism	Red-Violet	B	Pisces
Alertness	Yellow	E	Mercury
Angina Pectoris	Yellow	E	Leo
Antiseptic	Blue	G#	Moon
	Blue-Violet	A	Saturn
Ankles	Violet	A#	Aquarius
Anemia	Yellow	E	Leo
Aneurism	Yellow	E	Leo
Anxiety	Blue	G#	Moon/Sagittarius
Anorexia	Blue	G#	Moon
Aorta problems	Yellow	E	Leo
Appendicitis	Yellow-Green	F	Virgo
Apoplexy	Red-Orange	C#	Taurus
Arms	Orange	D	Sun/Gemini
Arteries (Carotid)	Red-Orange	C#	Taurus
Arteries (hardening)	Yellow	E	Mercury/Leo
Arterio-sclerosis	Yellow	E	Leo
Arthritis	Red	C	Mars/Aries
Asphyxiation	Orange	D	Gemini
Asthma	Orange	D	Gemini
Ataxia	Blue	G#	Moon/Sagittarius
Blood (electrify)	Red	C	Mars/Aries
Bladder problems	Blue-Green	G	Scorpio
Blood (magnetize)	Blue	G#	Moon
Bronchitis	Orange	D	Sun/Gemini
Brain activity	Yellow	E	Mercury/Leo

128

Symptom	Color	Note	Stones
Brain stimulation	Green	F#	Venus
Breast	Yellow-Orange	D	Cancer
Bulimia	Blue	G#	Moon
Bunions	Red-Violet	B	Pisces
Cancer (bones)	Blue-Violet	A	Saturn/Capricorn
Cancer (brain)	Red	C	Mars/Aries
Cancer (skin)	Blue-Violet	A	Saturn/Capricorn
Cancer (throat)	Green	F#	Venus
Cancer (lung)	Yellow	F	Mercury
Cancer (stomach)	Violet	A#	Jupiter
Cancer (sex organs)	Red	C	Mars
Calves	Violet	A#	Aquarius
Catarrh (nasal)	Blue-Green	G	Scorpio
Cerebral disease	Red	C	Aries
Cervical Vertebrae	Red-Orange	C#	Taurus
Circulation (balance)	Violet	A#	Jupiter
Coma	Red	C	Mars/Aries
Colon (lower)	Blue-Green	G	Scorpio
Constipation	Red-Orange	C#	Taurus
	Blue-Green	G	Scorpio
Congestion	Yellow	E	Mercury
Cough	Yellow-Green	F	Virgo
	Orange	D	Sun/Gemini
Courage	Yellow	E	Leo
	Red	C	Mars/Aries
Creativity	Green	F#	Venus/Libra
Croup	Red-Orange	C#	Taurus
Deafness	Red-Orange	C#	Taurus
Depression	Yellow-Orange	D#	Cancer
Diaphragm	Yellow-Orange	D#	Cancer
Dizziness	Green	F#	Libra
Digestive upsets	Blue	G#	Moon
Dropsy	Yellow-Orange	D	Cancer
	Violet	A#	Jupiter
Drug addiction	Red-Violet	B	Pisces

Symptom	Color	Note	Stones
Ears	Red-Orange	C#	Taurus
Eczema	Blue-Violet	A	Saturn/Capricorn
	Green	F#	Venus
	Yellow-Green	F	Virgo
Emotional balance	Yellow	E	Leo
Energy	Red	C	Mars
	Yellow	E	Mercury
Epilepsy	Blue-Violet	A	Saturn/Capricorn
	Red	C	Mars
	Blue	G#	Moon
Esophagus	Yellow-Orange	D#	Cancer
Exhaustion	Red-Violet	B	Pisces
Eyes	Red	C	Aries
Fainting spells	Red	C	Mars/Aries
Fear	Orange	D	Sun
	Yellow	E	Leo
Feet	Red-Violet	B	Pisces
Fertility	Green	F#	Venus
	Blue-Green	G	Scorpio
Gallstones	Yellow-Orange	D	Cancer
Gas	Yellow-Orange	D#	Cancer
Genito-urinary tract	Blue-Green	G	Scorpio
Gout	Red-Violet	B	Pisces
Goiter	Red-Orange	C#	Taurus
Hands	Orange	D	Gemini
Headache	Red	C	Aries
Head cold	Blue-Green	G	Scorpio
Heart inflammation	Orange	D	Sun
Heart palpitation	Violet	A#	Jupiter/Aquarius
Heart pain	Yellow	E	Leo
Heart irregularity	Violet	A#	Jupiter/Aquarius
Hernia	Blue-Green	G	Scorpio
Hiccoughs	Yellow-Orange	D#	Cancer
Hips	Blue	G#	Sagittarius
Hypothermia	Red	C	Mars

Symptom	Color	Note	Stones
Hysteria	Yellow-Orange	D#	Cancer
Iliac arteries	Blue	G#	Moon
Indigestion	Yellow-Orange	D#	Cancer
Infertility (female)	Green	F#	Venus/Taurus
Infertility (male)	Red	C	Mars/Aries
Influenza	Yellow-Green	F	Virgo
	Red-Violet	B	Pisces
Intelligence	Yellow	E	Mercury
Insomnia	Blue	G#	Moon
Intestines	Yellow-Green	F	Virgo
Intuition	Red-Orange	C#	Taurus
Jaw (lower)	Red-Orange	C#	Taurus
Jaundice	Yellow-Green	F	Virgo
	Red-Violet	B	Pisces
Kidneys	Violet	A#	Jupiter
Kidneys (inflammation)	Green	F#	Libra
Kidney stones	Blue-Green	G	Scorpio
Knees	Blue-Violet	A	Capricorn
Larynx	Red-Orange	C#	Taurus
Legs	Blue-Violet	A	Capricorn
Leprosy	Blue-Violet	A	Saturn
Liver	Red-Violet	B	Pisces
	Yellow-Green	F	Virgo
Liver (upper lobes)	Yellow-Orange	D#	Cancer
Love	Green	F#	Venus
Lumbago	Green	F#	Libra
Lungs	Orange	D	Gemini
Malignant tumors	Blue-Violet	A	Saturn
Malnutrition	Yellow-Green	F	Virgo
	Red-Violet	B	Pisces
Mania	Blue	G#	Moon
Menses (irregular)	Red-Orange	C#	Taurus
	Blue-Green	G	Scorpio
Menses (late)	Red-Orange	C#	Taurus
Menses (profuse)	Blue-Green	G	Scorpio

Symptom	Color	Note	Stones
Mental fatigue	Orange	D	Sun/Gemini
Mood disorders	Blue	G#	Moon
Mumps	Red-Orange	C#	Taurus
Muscle fatigue	Red	C	Mars/Aries
Nasal polyps	Red-Orange	C#	Taurus
Nausea	Yellow-Orange	D#	Cancer
	Blue-Violet	A	Capricorn
Neck	Orange	D	Gemini
	Yellow	E	Mercury
	Red-Orange	C#	Taurus
	Green	F#	Venus
Nervousness	Blue	G#	Moon
Neuralgia	Red	C	Mars
Neuritis	Orange	D	Gemini
	Yellow-Green	F	Virgo
Nose	Blue-Green	G	Scorpio
Ovaries	Blue-Green	G	Scorpio
Palate	Red-Orange	C#	Taurus
Pancreas	Yellow-Green	F	Virgo
Panic disorder	Blue	G#	Moon
Passion	Red	C	Mars
Peritonitis	Yellow-Green	F	Virgo
Pleurisy	Orange	D	Sun/Gemini
Pneumonia	Yellow-Orange	D#	Cancer
	Orange	D	Sun/Gemini
	Yellow-Green	F	Virgo
Prosperity	Green	F#	Venus
Prostate	Red-Orange	C#	Taurus
Psychic development	Blue	G#	Moon
	Violet	A#	Jupiter
	Blue-Violet	A	Saturn
Rectum	Blue-Green	G	Scorpio
Reproductive system	Blue-Green	G	Scorpio
Rheumatism	Orange	D	Sun/Gemini
	Blue	G#	Sagittarius

Symptom	Color	Note	Stones
Sciatica	Blue	G#	Sagittarius
Schizophrenia	Blue	G#	Moon
Security	Blue-Violet	A	Saturn/Capricorn
Shoulders	Orange	D	Gemini
Skin (inflammation)	Green	F#	Venus/Libra
Sneezing (excessive)	Yellow-Green	F	Virgo
	Orange	D	Gemini
Speech	Yellow-Green	F	Virgo
Spinal cord	Yellow	E	Leo
Spinal meningitis	Yellow	E	Leo
Spine (inflammation)	Violet	A#	Aquarius
Spine (lower)	Yellow-Green	F	Virgo
Spine (curvature)	Yellow	E	Leo
Spleen	Yellow-Green	F	Virgo
Stimulation (general)	Red	C	Mars
Strength	Red	C	Mars
	Orange	D	Sun
Stomach	Blue-Violet	A	Capricorn
Stomach (tumor)	Blue-Violet	A	Capricorn
	Yellow-Orange	D#	Cancer
Suprarenals	Green	F#	Libra
Temperature (high)	Blue	G#	Moon/Sagittarius
Temperature (low)	Red	C	Mars
Temperature (normal)	Yellow	E	Mercury
Thighs	Blue	G#	Sagittarius
Thoracic duct	Yellow-Orange	D#	Cancer
Throat	Red-Orange	C#	Taurus
Tobacco addiction	Red-Violet	B	Pisces
Tonsillitis	Red-Orange	C#	Taurus
Toothache	Blue	G#	Moon
Tuberculosis	Orange	D	Sun/Gemini
Tumors	Blue-Violet	A	Saturn/Capricorn
Ulcers	Blue-Violet	A	Capricorn
	Yellow-Orange	D#	Cancer
Uremia	Green	F#	Libra

Symptom	Color	Note	Stones
Urethra	Blue-Green	G	Scorpio
Vaginitis	Red-Orange	C#	Taurus
Varicose veins	Violet	A#	Sagittarius
Vision	Red	C	Aries
Water retention	Violet	A#	Jupiter
Womb	Blue-Green	G	Scorpio
Worry	Red-Violet	B	Pisces
Wounds	Blue-Violet	A	Saturn
Worms	Blue-Violet	A	Capricorn
	Blue-Green	G	Scorpio

PART TWO

PART TWO

8

A STONE ENCYCLOPEDIA

CRYSTALS, GEMS, AND MINERALS FOR THE NEW MILLENNIUM
This section contains an alphabetical listing of one hundred or more crystals, gems, and minerals. The arrangement is easy to follow. First, the stone is listed by its proper or common name. The crystal system in which the stone is found comes next, followed by the cell salt, color, energy, astrological attribution (see the section titled "The Planets" in chapter 1 or "The Seven Spirit Energy Centers" in chapter 4, for additional information) and stone lore. Finally we get into the medicine uses inherent in the stone.

Editor's Note: The 16-page color section included in this volume (between pages 72–73) illustrates many of the stones listed here. These stones are marked with an asterisk.

I have attempted to include as much information regarding each stone as possible; however, some of the entries contain more information than others. If you want to know what a particular stone looks like, get yourself a copy of *The Audubon Society Field Guide to American Rocks and Minerals* (New York: The Audubon Society, 1978)—it's an excellent resource book and guide. Also, keep in mind that while I've provided traditional, contemporary, and subjective accounts of the healing properties embodied in stones, how a stone "feels" as well as how it may be used is ultimately up to you. For example, I have listed the astrological attributions in accordance with the six crystal systems; however, you may also work with stones through color if you choose. I suggest that you use the following interpretations as a reference guide only, and make the effort to become personally familiar with the stone spirits in your possession. Meanwhile, happy crunching....

ABALONE (see SEA SHELL)*

AGATE (see CHALCEDONY)*

ALMANDINE (see GARNET)*

AMBER*

Crystal System: Amber is amorphous, and not linked with any specific system

Cell Salt: No specific cell salt; amber is a fossil resin found in alluvian soils, coniferous trees, and on some seashores

Color: Translucent yellow, honey-colored, or brownish yellow with mummified insect and/or plant inclusions

Energy: Electric

Element: Fire

Planet/Sign: Sun/Leo; Mercury

Stone Lore: Amber is a very old mineral substance; amber talismans have been found in Stone Age archaeological deposits. Because this material is easily worked, it was often shaped into jewelry, amulets, or pipestems, and traded among various ancient European peoples.

The roughly marked, circular depressions found in natural amber were thought to be the resting places of the spirits that animated the stone. When carved into animal forms or marked by Nature in this way, amber contained special power, and could transfer that power to the bearer of the stone.

Medicine Uses: Amber may be used to increase vitality, motivation, and creativity. It is a powerful amulet when worn for protection, especially when carved in the shape of your totem animal.

Wear amber to attract warm, loyal, and generous people into your life; or carry amber on your person to lend logic or wit to a difficult situation.

Mixed with turquoise, amber is reminiscent of Sky Father or the sun in the sky. This combination of energies may be used successfully to quiet the mind and calm the nervous system.

Knock on wood three times with a natural piece of amber to call on the spirits of the trees for special favors.

To increase prosperity, sew amber and turquoise along with several coins into a coyote skin pouch and bury the pouch in the earth.

AMETHYST (see QUARTZ)*

ANDRADITE (see GARNET)

ANHYDRITE

Crystal System: Orthorhombic

Cell Salt: Calcium sulphate

Color: Ranges from white, gray, blue, red, or brick red to lavender; may appear translucent or fluorescent

Energy: Electric

Element: Fire

Planet/Sign: Mars-Pluto/Scorpio (exact cell salt equivalent); also Venus/Taurus; Sun/Leo

Stone Lore: Anhydrite may be associated with the contemporary Slavic shaman belief that the first rudiments of future souls are created through energy initially borne in crystals, gems, and minerals, because this is a remarkable transformative stone.

Medicine Uses: The main function of anhydrite is to assist in breaking down old habit patterns by bringing secrets buried deep within the soul to light. This stone will also open the heart center by arousing sympathy for the human condition.

ANT HILL CRYSTALS*

Crystal System: Hexagonal

Cell Salt: Silicon Dioxide

Color: Clear; sometimes translucent; milky white or beige

Energy: Electric

Element: Fire

Planet/Sign: Sagittarius

Stone Lore: Ant hill crystals may be found anywhere, as ants bring them up to the surface of the Earth during the formation of ant hills. North and South American shamans use ant hill crystals in their medicine bags and rattles in order to remain in contact with the spirits.

Medicine Uses: Ant hill crystals expand and awaken the mind and soul through memory. These stones may be found at any ant hill; the bigger the ants, the larger the crystals.

Try this ant hill crystal medicine: gather ant hill crystals, remembering to ask permission and thank the ants. Create your own rattle (an empty aluminum soft drink can works wonders). Place the ant hill crystals inside and shake it about the house to clear a negative atmosphere. Or shake the rattle around your aura to clear out old emotional debris. The rattle may also be used for protection; the sound made by the ant hill crystals keeps evil spirits at bay.

ANTIMONY*
Crystal System: Orthorhombic

Cell Salt: Native, sometimes containing arsenic, iron, and silver

Color: Tin-white to light steel-gray.

Energy: Electric

Element: Fire

Planet/Sign: Sun/Leo

Stone Lore: Antimony is rare in North America, although it has been found in California. It is commonly mined in Mexico and Canada.

Medicine Uses: This metallic mineral may be worn against the skin for vitality, protection, and improved circulation.

ANTLER (see BONE)*

APACHE TEARS (see OBSIDIAN)*

APATITE
Crystal System: Hexagonal

Cell Salt: Calcium-fluorine-hydroxyl phosphate, often with small amounts of manganese and cerium

Color: Varying hues of green, brown, red, yellow, violet, and pink, as well as white and clear

Energy: Electromagnetic

Element: Fire, Air, and Earth

Planet/Sign: Jupiter/Sagittarius; Mercury/Virgo

Stone Lore: Apatite is found all over North America, as well as in Mexico, Norway, Russia, and Sri Lanka.

Medicine Uses: Apatite is a "mind over matter" stone. It helps to quiet emotional upset, especially during the more difficult phases of transformative deepening, such as divorce and death.

The influence of the green, brown, red, violet, pink, white, and clear stones is dissolving, while pale yellow apatite crystals are resolving.

APHTITALITE

Crystal System: Hexagonal

Cell Salt: Potassium sulphate, often with other elements

Color: Colorless or white

Energy: Neutral; magnetic

Element: Air and Fire

Planet/Sign: Mercury/Virgo (exact cell salt equivalent); also Jupiter/ Sagittarius

Stone Lore: None available

Medicine Uses: Aphtitalite may be used to promote unity and harmony in the body, mind, and soul, as this stone balances the flow of cosmic energy throughout the body-earth. Use aphtitalite when you are feeling down, to encourage feelings of contentment and self-assurance.

APOPHYLLITE*

Crystal System: Tetragonal

Cell Salt: Hydrous calcium potassium fluorsilicate, often with a small amount of iron and nickel

Color: Ranges from clear to white, gray, green, yellow, and red, often with a pearly cast on cleavage

Energy: Magnetic

Element: Earth

Planet/Sign: Saturn/Capricorn; Mars/Aries; Mars-Pluto/Scorpio

Stone Lore: This stone is found in the North American states of New Jersey, Virginia, and Michigan, as well as in Mexico.

Medicine Uses: Use apophyllite crystal to re-evaluate spiritual, mental, emotional, and material resources and values. This stone brings victory through perseverance.

The clear and red crystals strengthen mental clarity and insight. Gray stones may be used to neutralize the opposition. Pale aqua or green apophyllite may work to alter the cellular consciousness of the body-earth by stimulating the reproductive organs through creative mental imagery.

AQUAMARINE (see BERYL)*

ARSENIC ☠

Crystal System: Hexagonal

Cell Salt: A native mineral ore, usually with some antimony, iron, nickel, silver, and sulphur

Color: Tin white, quickly tarnishing to dark gray; evolved specimens are orange-red with a metallic glow

Energy: Electric

Element: Fire, Air, and Earth

Planet/Sign: Jupiter/Sagittarius; Mercury/Virgo

Stone Lore: Arsenic crystal comes from England, France, Germany, and Italy. It has been found in small quantities in Arizona and British Columbia.

☠ **CAUTION: The fumes of arsenic crystal are poisonous, so take care to avoid breathing the fumes. Arsenic is deadly if taken internally.**

Medicine Uses: Despite the potential danger, this stone happens to be an excellent diagnostic tool for getting to the root of disruptive mental and physical conditions. It is especially beneficial when used to overcome inertia. The orange-red colored crystals are the preferred healing stones.

AUTUNITE

Crystal System: Tetragonal

Cell Salt: Hydrous phosphate of calcium and uranium, often with some barium and magnesium

Color: Strongly fluorescent; lemon to sulphur yellow, yellow-green or green

Energy: Magnetic

Element: Earth

Planet/Sign: Saturn/Capricorn (closest cell salt equivalent); Mars-Pluto/Aries

Stone Lore: Autunite is mined in Washington state, New Hampshire, North Carolina, and New Mexico.

Medicine Uses: Use autunite crystal to stimulate creative imagination as well as to bring the mind under conscious control and direction.

This crystal works to open up the sight center, thus enhancing the supersensory functions of hindsight, foresight, and insight.

Lemon yellow autunite crystals are most desirable for raising sexual energy to the heart level. Yellow-green and green crystals reflect Earth energy and may be used to concentrate love within the heart center.

Try this five-minute love medicine: Hold a yellow-green or green autunite crystal in the open palm of your receptive hand. Relax and breathe deeply, inhaling and exhaling through the nose. Now, drop your awareness to your heart and continue breathing through the heart center. Breathe in the love of Earth and all its creatures and things. Exhale love right back at them.

AVENTURINE (see QUARTZ)

AZURITE*

Crystal System: Monoclinic

Cell Salt: Basic copper carbonate

Color: Azure blue to dark blue; glassy and low-lustered

Energy: Magnetic

Element: Water

Planet/Sign: Moon; Venus; Jupiter/Pisces

Stone Lore: Azurite is commonly found in Arizona.

Medicine Uses: Azurite crystals calm the emotional/auric energy field surrounding the body-earth. Wear azurite against the skin to produce sensations of empathy, compassion, and love.

Deep azure blue specimens are favored for developing psychic abilities through the pituitary center or third eye. Combined with malachite crystal, azurite may be used to soothe extreme anxiety affecting the back portion of the brain. It is thus an excellent alternative treatment for conditions such as anxiety attacks, panic disorder, anorexia, and bulimia.

BARITE*

Crystal System: Orthorhombic

Cell Salt: Barium sulphate, with small amounts of strontium

Color: White, gray, or colorless; or, yellow, brownish red, or blue, with a vitreous and pearly luster

Energy: Electromagnetic

Element: Earth and Fire

Planet/Sign: Venus/Taurus; Sun/Leo; Mars-Pluto/Scorpio

Stone Lore: Barite crystal is primarily mined in the North American states of California, Colorado, and South Dakota.

Medicine Uses: Barite crystal is a strong muscle stimulant. It may be used to alleviate the chills caused by hypothermia, fever, and inflammation due to the agreeable sense of warmth it produces when placed in contact with the body.

Use barite to raise your spirits during depression; laughter may occur if the stone is held in the receptive hand long enough.

Try using barite crystal during shamanic journey work or astral travel; this stone causes some sensitive individuals to feel as though they could fly through the air.

BERYL*

Crystal System: Hexagonal

Cell Salt: Beryllium aluminum silicate, frequently with sodium, lithium, and cesium

Color: Brilliant green (Emerald); blue, green-blue (Aquamarine); bright yellow (Golden Beryl); yellow-brown (Heliodor); red, pink (Morganite); white and colorless (Goshenite)

Energy: Electromagnetic

Element: Fire, Air, and Earth

Planet/Sign: Jupiter/Sagittarius, Mercury/Virgo

Stone Lore: Beryl is found in the United States, Mexico, Russia, Brazil, and India.

Beryl spheres or eggs were used for scrying during the Renaissance. The ancients used beryl in rain-making rituals. It is said that beryl was worn as protection against storms, drowning, and seasickness when traveling by water.

In the early 1200s, beryl was thought to help in courtroom litigation as well as on the battle field.

There is a "gem city" in Greek myth, called the City of the Islands of the Blessed, where beryl formed the temples of the Gods.

Medicine Uses: In general, beryl increases psychic awareness and heightens human potential by expanding the mind to grasp the laws of Nature. It quickens the mind, cures inertia, and rekindles romantic love in marital relationships.

This stone may also be used to enhance prophetic vision and to converse with water spirits.

There are many varieties of beryl crystal, usually categorized according to color. In all cases, beryl should be set in a silver necklace, or set in silver and worn on the left ring finger.

AQUAMARINE* crystal fosters acceptance of the transient nature of physical existence. The deep oceanic shades of aqua are best for transmutative purposes, and may ease us through the processes of death. This stone offers protection and courage. Pale blue or blue-green stones afford the wearer soothing calm.

Aquamarine is the ultimate water divination stone: place it in a crystal bowl filled with pure, natural spring water. Gaze deeply into the bowl and allow the images engendered through the stone to flow freely into consciousness.

Drink aquamarine water as a tonic, to enhance psychic awareness and mental clarity.

EMERALD* is perhaps the most popular and highly prized beryl crystal. Brilliant green emerald is an Earth Mother stone, a stone of Nature, and therefore heightens our ability to be ecology-conscious.

Creative imagination, prosperity, protection, love, and fertility are increased by emerald crystal. Wear an emerald ring on the index finger of your receptive hand to relieve or prevent disease, or against the throat to gently calm and balance all seven spirit energy centers at once.

Gaze at the emerald to soothe tired eyes, or keep emerald crystal in the northernmost corner of the home to keep out evil spirits.

The best emerald crystals come from India. Choose specimens that are colored medium to dark transparent green or blue-green. Inclusions are common and do not negatively affect the quality of the stone.

GOLDEN BERYL stimulates the heart, clears the mind, and promotes genuine feelings of love and affection when worn in a ring on the third finger of the Sun or the fourth finger of Mercury on the receptive hand.

GOSHENITE is a memory stone. White goshenite may be used to clear long-held emotional patterns lingering in the psyche; colorless goshenite crystal assists in bringing the spirit of the cosmos to earth-plane consciousness.

Use goshenite to remember past lives and bless the ancestors: hold goshenite in the open palm of your receptive hand. Breathe deeply and focus your attention behind you. Begin to pray for your relatives—first the living, then the dead. Follow the ancestral stream, allowing the images of family members to appear in your mind's eye. Bless and forgive each image that arises to the surface. Now hold the stone against your solar plexus as you bless and forgive yourself.

HELIODOR crystal may be used as an aid to concentration when working to manifest a specific goal. Plant raw, yellow-brown heliodor at the base of your favorite trees and shrubs and watch the plants grow tall and strong.

MORGANITE may help to resolve painful sexual issues regarding abuse and gender orientation. The purple-red stones accelerate self-forgiveness and self-love.

BLOODSTONE (see CHALCEDONY)

BOJI STONE

Crystal System: Isometric

Cell Salt: Trace metals and elements, including pyrite, palladium, fossil, and petrified bone

Color: Black, varying to lighter shades of metallic silver gray iridescence

Energy: Electric and magnetic

Element: Air and Water

Planet/Sign: Mercury/Gemini; Moon/Cancer; Saturn-Uranus/ Aquarius

Stone Lore: Boji stone comes from Kansas. It is a New Age stone.

Medicine Uses: Boji stone gathers energy within its powerful electromagnetic field. The smooth, round stones are "female," and the rough, crystallized, odd-shaped stones are "male." It is good to acquire a healing pair.

Boji stone balances energy and removes blockages from the aura as well as the body. It also cleans, charges, and fills up the holes in the aura.

Generally, this strange, heavy metallic ball is excellent for grounding subtle energies while establishing a harmonious polarity throughout the physical, emotional, mental and finer spirit bodies.

Boji stone works well when carried in a pouch on or about the person. Hold the stones in the fingers of your receptive hand along with rock crystal to neutralize bad vibes.

BONE*

Crystal System: None

Cell Salt: Calcium phosphate, calcium carbonate, calcium fluoride, calcium chloride, and magnesium phosphate, with small amounts of sodium chloride and sulphate

Color: Dull white, grayish white, brownish white, darker shades of brown

Energy: Magnetic

Element: Earth

Planet/Sign: Saturn/Capricorn

Stone Lore: Bone comprises the skeleton of most full-grown vertebrate animals, including humans. While not stone, bone has many similar elements, and is usually collected by rock hounds along with crystals, gems, and minerals.

Shamans use bones as part of their healing repertoire or as talismans and amulets. Some American Indian tribes use bones in healing ceremonies or purification rituals. Bone is also used to make needles and awls for sewing, arrow points, sled runners, knives, and tanning tools.

Medicine Uses: There are as many kinds of bones as there are fish, reptiles, birds, and animals. However, some types of bone are more popular or common than others.

ANTLER* is used to rake the Grandfather rocks into the fire pit during certain Native American sweat lodge ceremonies. Deer antler is commonly worn in a headdress by shamans or tribal dancers. The antlers of elk, moose, and deer are used for decorative purposes as well. Antler is strong hunting medicine, as this bone calls the spirit of the animal to the hunter.

In European myth, the antler is a symbol of Cernunnos, the Horned God, who is lord of the forest.

BIRD BONE is used by shamans of various cultures to call upon the spirits of the upper world. In the North American Plains Indian tradition, eagle-bone represents peace. Fashioned into a whistle, its piercing cry blows away harmful energies on the wind. The eagle-bone whistle also blows our thoughts and prayers to the Great Spirit and catches spirit songs out of the air.

Hawk bone is very powerful medicine for eliminating specific illnesses in the body because the hawk is a strong hunter and brings understanding.

Owl bone can be used for good or ill, depending on the intentions of the practitioner. It is helpful for understanding secrets and the deeper mysteries of life.

HOOF is commonly used to make rattles or pendants, or hatchets or mallets for butchering.

HORNS are used for curing blood diseases, as blood-sucking cups, and for headresses, as well as for spoon ladles, wedges for splitting wood, and bow-making.

IVORY* comes from whales, walruses, and elephants. This highly prized bone is rare, as the creatures that have died to gift us with it are endangered or near extinction. It has long been a favorite for jewelry and talismanic adornments. Never acquire ivory for aesthetic purposes. Use it only if it has great spiritual significance for you; otherwise, forget it. However, if you find that ivory happens to come into your possession, make many offerings to the animal spirit who gave its life for you.

Ivory is a sacred bone and should be revered as such. It is good for arthritic conditions and all ailments of the bones and teeth.

CALCITE*

Crystal System: Hexagonal

Cell Salt: Calcium carbonate

Color: White or colorless; pale shades of gray, yellow, red, blue, and green; black to brown when impure

Energy: Electromagnetic

Element: Air and Fire

Planet/Sign: Mercury/Virgo; Jupiter/Sagittarius

Stone Lore: Calcite is a common stone found all over North America.

Calcite, sometimes known as Iceland Spar, was once used by the Norse as a sun stone, as well as a divinatory tool to help navigate a course for ships at sea. It is still used as a healing stone by traditional Pennsylvania Dutch healers, who call it the "divinity stone."

Medicine Uses: Evolved specimens of calcite crystal are clear and reflective, like a magic mirror. Clear calcite crystal refracts light and doubles the energy of whatever it contacts. Gray calcite is a neutralizing agent.

Yellow calcite clears the mind. The red stones energize and tone the blood. Pink calcite opens the heart to receive affection and love. Blue crystals may be used during purification and healing rituals. Green calcite may be used as a money magnet or prosperity stone.

CATLINITE (see PIPESTONE)

CARNELIAN (see CHALCEDONY)

CATLINITE (see PIPESTONE)

CAT'S EYE QUARTZ (see QUARTZ)

CHALCEDONY*

Crystal System: Hexagonal

Cell Salt: Silicon dioxide

Color: White to gray, brown, blue, black; clear red to brownish red (Carnelian); bright green with red spots (Bloodstone/Heliotrope); variegated and banded (Agate); with mosslike or treelike inclusions (Moss Agate); apple-green (Chrysoprase); variegated and mottled red, yellow, brown (Jasper); whitish, dull gray, smoky brown to black (Flint)

Energy: Electric

Element: Air and fire

Planet/Sign: Mercury/Virgo; Jupiter/Sagittarius

Stone Lore: Chalcedony is found in Russia, India, Mexico, Brazil, and the United States.

Chalcedony is a form of quartz crystal. During the 1700s, it was believed that chalcedony embodied the power to banish evil spirits and nightmares. Like beryl, chalcedony was once carried by sailors to protect against drowning.

Astrologers of the Middle Ages wore engraved signet rings of chalcedony as amulets. The alchemist Paracelsus thought that chalcedony was a stone of the metal silver.

Magic stone fetishes made of chalcedony were fed sacrificial blood by some Burmese tribes, to guard the house and to keep the stones from eating the people.

Medicine Uses: In general, chalcedony gives success in lawsuits, good health, safe travels, and protects against harmful spirits. However, there are many varieties of chalcedony crystal, each with its own particular properties.

AGATE* is a stone of persuasion, attraction, harmony, and special attention. It gives courage, guards against danger and protects against worldly troubles. Hindu mystics believe that agate can help children overcome their fears, learn to walk earlier and maintain their balance. Set in a gold necklace, agate will quicken a sluggish metabolism.

Place variegated and banded agate crystals under your pillow at night to relieve insomnia and bring good dreams. Brown or black agates with a white ring in the center may be used to ward off the evil eye.

BLOODSTONE (HELIOTROPE) is a general healing stone and stimulant. Carry it to enrich iron-poor, tired blood or to help balance other blood-related disorders. Hold bloodstone against a bleeding wound to staunch the flow of blood.

The green, red-spotted bloodstone is also a prosperity stone; it ensures the wearer of monetary increase and abundant harvest. During the Middle Ages, bloodstone was thought to have the power to bring rain.

The bloodstone should be set in gold and worn around the neck near the heart.

CARNELIAN relieves sexual tension by redirecting the energy stored in the reproductive center of the body; it may also be used to excite sluggish sexual energy.

Unresolved feelings of anger, hostility, and hatred may be harmonized when carnelian is worn at the heart center, as this stone instills powerful sensations of well-being.

Like bloodstone, deep orange-red carnelian may help to staunch the flow of blood.

CHRYSOPRASE* feeds the heart and cleans the bloodstream of impurities by encouraging the proper assimilation and distribution of food-energy throughout the body-earth.

Pure, apple-green chrysoprase induces tranquility in nervous, high-strung dispositions, and can be helpful in the treatment of neurosis. This stone may also be used to reduce feverish or inflammatory conditions.

A chrysoprase crystal held in the mouth is said to grant the power of invisibility.

FLINT is considered to be a holy stone by many Native American tribes. It has been used for centuries to start the sacred fire, though with the coming of matches and cigarette lighters, many young people have forgotten how to create sparks with flint.

Learn to make fire with flint. Set up a fire ring in a safe place. Gather up some kindling (shredded newspaper, straw, dried twigs). Pray to the stone spirits and ask them to help you. Then knock two flints together until you make sparks that catch the kindling on fire. Enjoy the flames and reflect on feelings of gratitude for the heat and light, gifts of Father Sky and Mother Earth. Share your knowledge with others so the tradition will not be forgotten.

Ancient blades of flint have been found throughout Europe. Flint knives are still in use today for magical invocation and protection.

Carve a flint blade. Cast a magic circle in the dirt (or symbolically on the living room floor) with the blade, beginning in the east and moving clockwise south, west, and north, back to east. To divine the future, place the blade on its side in the middle of the circle and set it spinning in a clockwise motion. Note where the blade is pointing when the spinning stops. East is the future place, west is the past, north represents mystery, and south is fulfillment in the here and now.

JASPER* works directly on the animal soul to heighten and intensify primal awareness. It is both a divinatory and a "karmic" stone, and may be used to control psychic reactions and automatic responses.

Some Native American tribes use jasper to make rain. This stone may also cure snake bite by drawing venom from the wound.

Red jasper may be worn for protection. Clear the mind with yellow jasper. Brown jasper is an aid to concentration and may be worn for centering and grounding.

MOSS AGATE is a beautiful stone, with mossy, treelike inclusions. It can be used as a touchstone to enhance ecology-consciousness. Moss agate gives an eye for beauty; wear it during gardening and landscaping projects to increase the beauty of your surroundings.

ONYX* registers the gravitational pull of Earth. It therefore is grounding, aids concentration, and absorbs negativity from the environment. Use onyx when there is a need for protection, self-discipline, or sexual self-control.

When you wish to dissolve a particular relationship, wear onyx crystal close to your heart or present a gift of onyx to the other person.

CHRYSOBERYL

Crystal System: Orthorhombic

Cell Salt: Beryllium aluminum oxide, often with small amounts of iron and chromium

Color: Yellow-green to deep green; blue-green (Alexandrite); green-white, green-brown and yellow (Cat's Eye)

Energy: Magnetic and electric

Element: Earth and Fire

Planet/Sign: Venus/Taurus; Sun/Leo; Mars-Pluto/Scorpio

Stone Lore: The finest specimens of chrysoberyl come from Ceylon, where the stone is highly prized as a charm against evil spirits.

Medicine Uses: Chrysoberyl raises sexual energy from the lower bodily centers up to the heart level. It enables the wearer to respond to others with genuine feelings of kindness and affection.

ALEXANDRITE encourages receptivity and surrender to the forces of Nature. Blue-green alexandrite teaches self-discipline and control; it may also bring luck in love as it harmonizes opposing male and female energies within the relationship.

CAT'S EYE is an ancient Asian stone with many uses. The uppermost branches of the Hindu world tree were said to be made of cat's eye, hinting that this stone may be used to see into the future or communicate with the spirit world.

Cat's eye has long been touted as a health and beauty aid; place a cat's eye in spring water overnight and drink the liquid in the morning as a tonic. As this stone epitomizes the phrase "live long and prosper," wear cat's eye to increase longevity as well as to bring prosperity.

CHRYSOPRASE (see CHALCEDONY)*

CHRYSOCHOLLA*

Crystal System: Monoclinic

Cell Salt: Basic copper silicate

Color: Green, blue-green; brown to black (from impurities in the stone)

Energy: Magnetic

Element: Earth and Water

Planet/Sign: Venus-Neptune/Pisces

Stone Lore: Chrysocholla is mined in Mexico, Zaire, Chile, Russia, and the United States.

Medicine Uses: Chrysocholla works directly on the cells of the body to heal inflammation and disease.

Use chrysocholla to bless the past and forgive old hurts and disappointments. This will release the cells that hold onto sickness, and clear the way for healthy new cells to regenerate the tissue and organs within the body-earth.

CHRYSOLITE (see PERIDOT)

CITRINE (see QUARTZ)*

CORAL (see SEA SHELL)

CORUNDUM*

Crystal System: Hexagonal

Cell Salt: Aluminum oxide

Color: White, gray; brown to black; deep red (Ruby); blue (Sapphire); black, from a mixture of magnetite, hematite or spinel (Emery)

Energy: Electric

Element: Air and Fire

Planet/Sign: Mercury/Virgo; Jupiter/Sagittarius

Stone Lore: Corundum was among seven stone amulets worn for protection by the sea-faring people of ancient Greece. Rolled yellow and blue corundum pebbles have been found in streams down in Oaxaca, Mexico.

Medicine Uses: Corundum provides a cure for all the ills of the world. There are several colorful varieties of corundum, each with its own healing properties.

EMERY is a Saturn stone; use it for grounding and focusing your attention on a particular subject. This black stone is also an excellent aid for self-evaluation; it will help you get to the root of the problem fast.

RUBY* gives a general sense of well-being throughout the body-earth. It can remove evil thoughts and worry, control the sexual appetite, and resolve disputes.

The Chinese believe the ruby confers long life. To dream of ruby suggests great joy and good fortune.

Ruby was once thought to make the wearer invulnerable to wounds, especially if the skin was pierced with the stone. Wear ruby on the left side of the body, or on the index or little finger of the receptive hand, as a shield against misfortune; or incorporate ruby jewelry as a body-piercing adornment for added protection and power.

The ruby develops a sympathetic rapport with the owner of the stone, and tends to fade in color if neglected for too long. Dark red rubies are "male," while the lighter stones are "female." Should you be drawn to ruby, try to acquire a mated pair.

For maximum strength, wear ruby on the left ring finger set in either gold or silver.

SAPPHIRE* lives in the roots of the Hindu world tree. It was once considered an ancestral stone, enabling the wearer to see into the world soul.

The sapphire represents wisdom, magnanimous thought, love, good manners, and vigilance. Kings once wore the sapphire around their necks to protect them from harm.

Because sapphire is a clear, pure blue color, like the sky, church fathers considered it to have a godly nature and it was therefore considered a "sacred" gem.

Sapphire has the power to influence the spirits; it is a tonic to counteract negative witchcraft and attract good spirits. It was therefore a great favorite among sorcerers. The star sapphire, which is milky or grayish blue, is the best guard against the evil eye. This stone may help to cure certain diseases of the physical eyes as well.

Ayurvedic healers recommend sapphire for diseases such as rheumatism, sciatica, neurological pain, epilepsy, hysteria, and all nerve disorders, especially when set in gold and worn around the neck.

Sapphire will sometimes change color if the person wearing the stone has an unfaithful nature. Gaze at this stone for several minutes as a preparation for meditation to help still and quiet a racing mind.

CRYSTAL (see QUARTZ)*

DIAMOND*

Crystal System: Isometric

Cell Salt: Carbon

Color: Colorless, clear; light yellow, brown, green, blue; deep brown, orange, violet, yellow, yellow-green, red, blue, deep green

Energy: Electric

Element: All

Planet/Sign: Saturn; Uranus; Mercury/Gemini; Moon/Cancer

Stone Lore: During the Middle Ages, diamond was thought to be a magic stone of great power. While this stone brought victory, strength, courage, and fortitude to the wearer, it was also believed that it could make the wearer unhappy. Perhaps this was because looking into the diamond was likened to gazing into the eye of the sun or the face of the gods. Likewise, the Hindus accorded power, friends, riches, good luck, youth, success, and death to the diamond.

In the Middle East, the diamond was a powerful talisman that could provoke shamanic ecstasy. Europeans found the first large "diamonds" in the leather bag of a South African sorcerer; however, it is more likely that these stones were actually rock crystals, the universal stone of choice among shamans.

Contemporary folklore states that it is better to receive a diamond as a gift than to purchase it; the stone supposedly has more power this way (and will save you a bundle of money, too!).

Medicine Uses: Attention, discrimination, recollection, receptivity, inspiration, faith, endurance, and concentration are the mental/emotional responses elicited via our relationship with diamond.

Because the diamond is capable of regenerating and reintegrating the body-earth, it may be worn as a reminder of our integral wholeness and spiritual perfection.

Diamond shields the wearer from negative projections and the manipulations of others. Try scrying with a diamond instead of a rock crystal ball to see into the future.

The diamond can be used as a heart tonic: place it in a glass of water overnight and drink the liquid the following day.

Pink or red diamond promotes feelings of love and affection. The blue diamond may bring tranquility into stressful situations. Green diamond has a soothing, calming effect on the central nervous system and the physical body in general. Breadth of vision and enthusiasm are inspired by violet diamond. Orange increases vital energy, while yellow enables the wearer to transmit healing light.

Diamond should be set in gold and worn on the right ring finger. Avoid low-quality diamonds, as these may have an adverse effect on your health.

DIOPSIDE

Crystal System: Monoclinic

Cell Salt: Calcium magnesium silicate

Color: White, colorless, gray, or green

Energy: Magnetic

Element: Earth and Water

Planet/Sign: Venus-Neptune/Pisces

Stone Lore: Diopside is found in Japan, Germany, Ireland, the United States, Russia, and India.

Medicine Uses: This mineral clears out congested emotions by circulating cosmic energy throughout the auric field.

Diopside increases creative visualization and helps to manifest desired goals. Clear or light green gem-quality crystals are preferred when using this stone for visionary purposes. Hold diopside on the third eye or pituitary center when formulating mental images and notice the clarity with which they appear.

Also, wear diopside against the skin between the throat and heart centers to attract love into your life.

DIOPTASE*

Crystal System: Hexagonal

Cell Salt: Basic copper silicate

Color: Deep vivid green

Energy: Magnetic

Element: Earth

Planet/Sign: Venus; Mercury/Virgo; Jupiter/Sagittarius

Stone Lore: This crystal is young in terms of evolutionary development. If dioptase crystal were left in the mines, it would eventually grow into emerald beryl.

Dioptase is the talismanic stone of the African Congo.

Medicine Uses: Dioptase crystal opens and expands the gateways of the mind. It prepares us to receive affection and love from all our relationships, the Earth, and the cosmos. Wear this stone to bring abundance, prosperity, creativity, peace, and good health into your life.

DRAVITE (see TOURMALINE)

ELBAITE (see TOURMALINE)*

EMERALD (see BERYL)*

EMERY (see CORUNDUM)

EPIDOTE

Crystal System: Monoclinic

Cell Salt: Basic calcium, aluminum, and iron silicate

Color: Yellow-green to brownish black

Energy: Magnetic

Element: Water

Planet/Sign: Neptune/Pisces; Virgo

Stone Lore: In eighteenth-century France and England, epidote was used in jewelry set with other gems to form a particular sentiment using the first letter of each stone. Epidote was the second "e" in the word "forever."

Medicine Uses: The epidote is a mediating influence, and may be carried on or about the person to ensure protection against conflicting circumstances. It soothes the emotional and physical bodies, stills fear, and lessens the frequency of panic and/or anxiety attacks.

Epidote also works to heal intestinal blockages due to nervous disorders affecting the stomach.

Epidote has recently entered a renewed stage of accelerated evolutionary growth and will soon be recognized as an important assistant in the self-healing process.

Greenish black and pistachio-colored stones are most favorable for reflecting, conducting, and projecting healing Earth energy back into the environment.

FLINT (see CHALCEDONY)

FLUORITE*

Crystal System: Isometric

Cell Salt: Calcium fluoride

Color: Violet, blue, green, yellow, brown, blue-black, pink, rose-red, colorless, and white

Energy: Electromagnetic

Element: Air and Water

Planet/Sign: Mercury/Gemini; Saturn-Uranus/Aquarius; Moon/Cancer (exact cell salt equivalent)

Stone Lore: Fluorite is a New Millennium stone.

Medicine Uses: The element of air predominates in this mineral substance. Use it to increase mental agility and when attempting to analyze important information.

This New Millennium stone emphasizes the concerns of ancestral connections, the immediate home and family, and our interconnectedness with the Earth. While fluorite impresses us on personal levels, it also conducts energy from the upper world of spirit to the lower world of soul. Generally, fluorite is helpful for easing emotional problems, especially those arising on the home front.

Fluorite is associated with fluoride, the tooth-decay preventative, and may be used to strengthen the teeth and bones.

Violet crystals promote mental expansion, allowing us to view ourselves and our actions from a higher vantage point. Blue fluorite benefits any situation requiring clear communication. Green fluorite may help to heal troubled relationships. Pink and rose-red stones are stimulating and revitalizing, and may be used to break down feelings of inertia. Brown or black crystals aid concentration, while the white or colorless varieties provide a protective shield of influence throughout the auric and physical bodies. Pictures and images held inside the stone, such as clouds, trees, or angels, also suggest the purpose of the stone in your possession.

FOOL'S GOLD (see PYRITE)*

GARNET*

Crystal System: Isometric

Cell Salt: Aluminum silicates (Pyrope, Almandine and Spessartine), and calcium silicates (Grossular, Andradite, and Uvarovite)

Color: Deep red to reddish black (Pyrope); deep red to brown or brownish black (Almandine); brownish red to hyacinth red (Spessartine); colorless, white, yellow, pink, green or brown (Grossular); wine red or greenish (Andradite); emerald green (Uvarovite)

Energy: Electromagnetic

Element: Air and Water

Planet/Sign: Mercury/Gemini; Moon/Cancer; Saturn-Uranus/ Aquarius

Stone Lore: Some Asiatic tribes once used garnets as bullets, believing that the red stone would cause a more deadly wound than a leaden bullet. An ancient Greco-Roman tradition claims that when engraved with the image of a dragon and worn as a talisman, the garnet brings riches, joy, and good health.

Medicine Uses: In general, garnet should be set in gold for individuals with nervous or sluggish dispositions, while active people should wear garnet set in silver.

ALMANDINE* was associated with Bacchus, the Roman god of wine. Tonic water prepared with almandine may be helpful in easing hangover symptoms. Place the stone in a bowl of purified water, let it stand overnight, and drink upon waking.

ANDRADITE unearths buried secrets. Take this stone with you when mining, beachcombing, or looking for lost objects. Give an andradite crystal to your lover and listen carefully to what he or she reveals to you.

GROSSULAR* increases our receptivity to the images held in Nature—sky, clouds, sun rays, moonbeams, and the green and growing things of Earth. This stone liberates the human spirit via its soothing, grounding, and calming effect on the emotional body.

PYROPE contains living fire and works to release outworn habit patterns by destroying the erroneous ideas and emotions that keep us enslaved to guilt and fear. Pyrope clears the way for new beginnings.

This stone has long been recognized for its use as an anti-inflammatory and blood-clotting agent.

SPESSARTINE inspires enthusiasm, refines one's manners, heightens awareness, sharpens the tongue, and lends personal grace and charm in dealings with the public.

UVAROVITE stands for growth, peace, prosperity, and abundance. Wear it against the lower belly as a fertility charm, or use it as a meditation aid to promote world peace.

GOLDEN BERYL (see BERYL)

GOSHENITE (see BERYL)

GROSSULAR (see GARNET)*

GYPSUM*

Crystal System: Monoclinic

Cell Salt: Hydrous calcium sulphate

Color: White, colorless (Selenite); gray, yellow, red or brown, with a pearlized luster on the cleavage of the stone

Energy: Magnetic

Element: Earth and Water

Planet/Sign: Venus-Neptune/Pisces

Stone Lore: Gypsum is highly prized in Russia, England, Japan, and Egypt. Russians and Egyptians cut golden yellow and salmon-colored gypsum into egg-shaped ornaments, ancient symbols of fertility.

Medicine Uses: Gypsum brings protection and good fortune. It is an excellent tool for developing mental telepathy.

SELENITE, the transparent variety of gypsum, may be used to strengthen and preserve the memory.

HALITE*

Crystal System: Isometric

Cell Salt: Sodium chloride (salt)

Color: Colorless or tinted with gray, yellow, red, or blue

Energy: Electromagnetic

Element: Fire

Planet/Sign: Jupiter/Sagittarius (exact cell salt equivalent); Mercury/Gemini; Moon/Cancer; Saturn-Uranus/Aquarius

Stone Lore: Halite is found in Germany and Austria as well as in the North American states of New York, Michigan, Kansas, and California.

The name "halite" comes from the Greek word *hals*, meaning "salt."

Medicine Uses: Halite crystal is actually solidified salt. Use it for grounding, protection, or to block negative energies.

If someone is wishing you harm, write his or her name nine times on a piece of white paper. Fold the paper into a small square and cover it completely with the halite cube. This won't hurt the other person, but it will stop them in their tracks when it comes to sending a bad hair day in your direction. For added protection, place a halite crystal in each of the the four corners of your house—north, south, east, and west.

HELIODOR (see BERYL)

HELIOTROPE (see CHALCEDONY)

HERKIMER DIAMOND (see QUARTZ)

HOOF (see BONE)

HOWLITE

Crystal System: Monoclinic

Cell Salt: Hydrated calcium silico-borate

Color: Dull, glimmering white

Energy: Magnetic

Element: Earth and Water

Planet/Sign: Venus-Neptune/Pisces

Stone Lore: Howlite is mined in Nova Scotia and California.

Medicine Uses: Howlite reflects and transfers spirit energy throughout the body-earth, and cleanses the mind and emotions of negative thoughts and images.

   This stone functions best when placed on a table or shelf, in close proximity to a well-frequented area.

HYACINTH (see ZIRCON)

INDICOLITE (see TOURMALINE)

IVORY (see BONE)*

JACINTH (see ZIRCON)

JADE (JADEITE or NEPHRITE)*

Crystal System: Monoclinic

Cell Salt: Sodium aluminum silicate, often with some calcium and iron

Color: Yellow, apple green, emerald green (Imperial Jade) to white and translucent (Jadeite)

Energy: Magnetic

Element: Earth and Water

Planet/Sign: Venus-Neptune/Pisces

Stone Lore: Jade comes primarily from the Orient.

Jadeite was a magical stone of Xiuhtecuhtli, the Aztec god of fire. It was also a favorite body-piercing stone of the indigenous inhabitants of Brazil and the West Indies, and highly prized as a remedy by Egyptian healers. Axe heads and other tools of jade have been found in archeological sites throughout the world.

Medicine Uses: American Indians use jade to heal all ailments associated with the kidneys as well as to aid in childbirth. Jade may be worn when treating gallstones, the lungs, the heart, and the throat as well.

Set in gold and silver jewelry, jade is thought to prolong life and bring abundant riches to the wearer.

A Chinese tonic made of powdered jade, rice, and rainwater, when boiled in a copper pot and carefully filtered through a fine mesh to remove all impurities, may strengthen the muscles, harden the bones, quiet the mind, tone the skin, and clean the blood. (Caution: Do not attempt this treatment without the guidance of a qualified ayurvedic professional.)

IMPERIAL JADE contains extremely powerful remedial abilities for clearing renal disorders due to its apple or emerald green coloring.

JARGOON (see ZIRCON)

JAROSITE

Crystal System: Hexagonal

Cell Salt: Basic hydrous potassium iron sulphate

Color: Cloudy amber, yellow, or dark brown

Energy: Electric

Element: Earth and Air

Antimony. This metallic mineral specimen sometimes contains arsenic, iron, and silver, and is difficult to distinguish from arsenic. It is used for vitality, protection, and improved circulation.

Calcite. This crystal was once used by the Norse as a sun stone and a divination tool to help ships navigate at sea. Yellow calcite clears the mind.

Smithsonite. (Inyo County, California) This mineral, a source of zinc, enhances our ability to reach our goals, and is useful in settling disputes. It will help clarify the mind and instill a sense of security.

Rhodochrosite. (Catamarca, Argentina) An ore of Manganese, rhodochrosite is useful in treating circulatory or lung-related problems. A crystal under your pillow at night will help you remember your dreams.

Barite. (Missouri) This crystal is a strong muscle stimulant. It may be used to alleviate chills or raise your spirits during depression, and can also be used during shamanic journey work or astral travel. If held long enough it can make you laugh.

Chrysocolla. This crystal works directly on the cells of the body to heal inflammation and disease. Use to bless the past and forgive old hurts.

Apophyllite. (Centreville, Fairfax County, Virginia) This crystal brings victory through perseverance. Use to re-evaluate resources and values.

Azurite. (Grant County, New Mexico) This stone is usually found in the upper layers of copper deposits. Deep blue is favored for developing psychic abilities.

Aquamarine. (Pakistan) This beryl crystal fosters acceptance of the transient nature of existence and brings calmness.

Beryl.
(Minas Gerais, Brazil) Beryl increases psychic awareness, and can be used to enhance prophetic vision.

Emerald. (Colombia) Creativity, love, and fertility are increased by this beryl crystal. Kept in the northern-most corner of a home, it may ward off evil spirits.

Crazy Lace Agate. Variegated forms of chalcedony such as these can relieve insomnia and bring good dreams if placed under your pillow.

Agate. There are many varieties of chalcedony, each with its own properties. Agate, when set in gold, will quicken the wearer's sluggish metabolism.

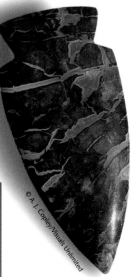

Agate. This variation of the chalcedony family is a stone of persuasion and harmony. It gives courage and guards against danger.

Jasper. (Cave Creek, Arizona) This chalcedony variety is both a divinatory and a karmic stone. Some native tribes use jasper to make rain.

Onyx. (Baja, Mexico) This chalcedony crystal absorbs negativity from the environment. It should be used for grounding and protection.

Turntell Agate. A variation of chalcedony with small seashell inclusions. Like beryl, chalcedony was once carried by sailors to protect against drowning.

Chrysoprase. A variation of chalcedony, chrysoprase crystal induces tranquility and can be useful in treating nervous conditions.

Petrified Wood. (Brunswick County, North Carolina) This is a very old stone and a record keeper for the earth. Because trees have a circulatory system as do humans, petrified wood may be used as a remedy for skin, circulation, and muscle problems.

Ant Hill Crystals. These can be found anywhere as ants bring the crystals to the surface. This pebble ants' nest was photographed at Wheeler Peak, Nevada. North and South American shamans use these crystals in medicine bags and rattles to remain in contact with the spirits.

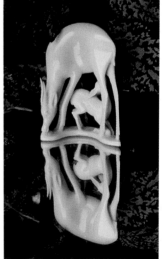

Antler. The antler and portion of the skull of a white-tail deer (*odocoileus virginianus*). The antler might be used to draw rocks through the coals of a fire during Native American sweat lodge ceremonies.

Ivory. (Kinshasha, Zaire, Africa) Ivory is becoming increasingly rare as the animals that produce it are endangered or near extinction. As a sacred bone it should be revered, and used only if it has great spiritual significance.

Sapphire. A deep blue example of the corundum group—the Luzon sapphire. This crystal represents wisdom, love, magnanimous thought, good manners, and vigilance.

© A. J. Copley/Visuals Unlimited

© Dane S. Johnson/Visuals Unlimited

Ruby. The red member of the corundum group, the ruby can remove evil thoughts and resolve disputes.

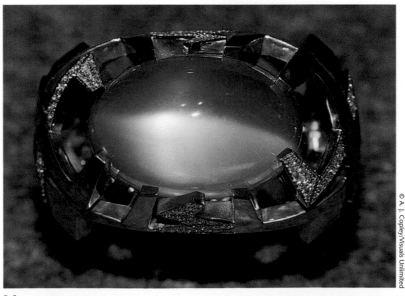

© A. J. Copley/Visuals Unlimited

Moonstone. Due to the moving spirit-light inside this stone, it may be used in scrying, hypnotherapy, or divination. Some moonstones can be used to mark the waxing and waning of the moon.

Diamond. (Kelsey Lake, Colorado) This is a .203 ct. near-colorless diamond. Diamond shields the wearer from negative projections and may be used as a heart stone.

Dioptase. (Mindouli, Zaire, Africa) Wear dioptase to bring abundance, creativity, and good health to your life.

Dioptase. (Namibia, Africa) Dioptase is the talismanic stone of the African Congo. It opens and expands the gateways of the mind.

© Ross Frid 1997/Visuals Unlimited

© A. J. Copley/Visuals Unlimited

Grossular. (Asbeston, Canada) This specimen of the garnet group soothes and calms the emotions, and fosters an appreciation of Nature.

© Ken Lucas/Visuals Unlimited

Pyrite. (Utah) Polished pyrite is an excellent divination tool. Mexican Indians make scrying mirrors from pyrite.

Almandine. (Wrangell Island, Alaska) A variety of garnet, almandine was associated with Bacchus, God of Wine. It can be helpful in easing hangovers.

© Ken Lucas/Visuals Unlimited

Fluorite. (Cave-in-Rock, Illinois) Fluorite is known as a new millennium stone, and emphasizes our interconnectedness with earth. In general it is helpful in easing emotional problems.

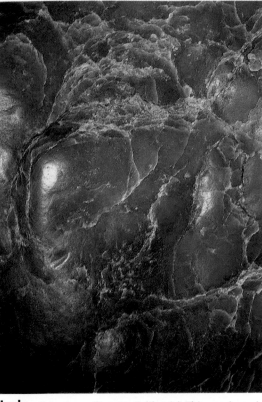

Halite. This crystal, NaCl-Sodium Chloride, is actually solidified salt. A halite crystal placed in each corner of your house will protect you from harm.

Lazurite. Also known as lapis lazuli, lazurite is part of the sodalite group of minerals. This stone was traditionally carved into animal or bird forms and worn as jewelry to protect the wearer from harm. It is also effective in relieving depression or grief.

Jade. (Monterey County, California) This specimen is commonly known as jadeite or nephrite. Jade is often associated with healing kidney ailments. When worn as jewelry, jade is thought to prolong life and enrich the wearer.

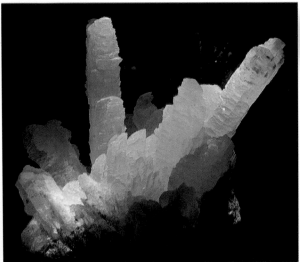

Gypsum. This is an excellent tool for improving memory and developing mental telepathy. It brings good fortune.

Malachite. (Zaire, SW Africa) Malachite can soothe and restore vitality, but because malachite tends to absorb negativity, it must be cleared and recharged after use.

Sodalite. This stone is a record-keeper, useful in memory work and receptive to new ideas and emotions. It combats the negative effects of radioactivity and is useful for balancing the metabolism.

© Arthur R. Hill
/Visuals Unlimited

Marcasite. (Gunajuato, Mexico) Crystals of marcasite have mind-calming and emotional stabilizing powers. Wear it set in silver for the best effect.

© Jeff J. Daly/Visuals Unlimited

© Ken Lucas/Visuals Unlimited

Malachite. (Bisbee, Cochise County, Arizona) This crystal has formed along with azurite crystals. Malachite can induce feelings of sympathy and compassion for others.

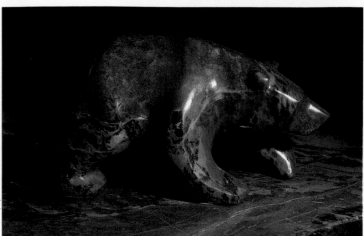

Rhodonite.
A "karma stone," rhodonite may accelerate the consequences of cause and effect. It encourages stability, moral courage, and is useful in monitoring behavior.

Obsidian. This variation, called snowflake obsidian, has gray-white inclusions. Obsidian can aid the decision-making process, and is excellent for grounding.

Apache Tears. This circular form of obsidian is often carried in a medicine pouch, or set in silver and worn as a powerful protective amulet.

Precious Opal. (Australia) This form of opal may be used in diagnostic and healing work. The color will fade if swept over a troublesome area.

© Charles Preitner/Visuals Unlimited

Pearls. A member of the sea shell family, pearls are created when an irritant is coated with calcium phosphate produced by the oyster. Pearls are useful in regulating body rhythms, and tend to absorb emotional energy, requiring clearing if exposed to a negatively charged situation.

Abalone. This member of the sea shell family is also known as the "ear shell." It is often used as a container for spirit offerings or smudging. It benefits the heart and digestion.

© A. J. Copley/ Visuals Unlimited

Tiger Cowrie. This distinctive sea shell (*cypread tigris*) is often used in jewelry and for decorating ceremonial garments. It carries the energy of the sea in offerings or in sympathetic magic.

© Don Fawcett/Visuals Unlimited

Amber. (Dominican Republic) The fossilized natural resins from ancient trees, amber is also found in alluvian soils and on some seashores. Wearing amber can attract generous and loyal people into your life.

© Ken Lucas/Visuals Unlimited

Rose Quartz. (Minas Gerais, Brazil) This stone exerts a soothing influence, calming emotions and healing traumatic memories. It makes an excellent gift for lovers, children, and anyone in need of sympathy and affection.

Amethyst. This variety of quartz crystal has marvelous healing powers. Hebrews believed it induced dreams and visions. Ancient Greeks thought it prevented drunkenness.

Tiger's Eye. The earth energy of this member of the quartz family is stabilizing and lends security to the wearer. Set in copper, it guards against harmful spirits.

Citrine. (Rio Grande de Sul, Brazil) A variety of quartz, citrine is energizing and positive. Used as a touchstone it will ease anxiety attacks and instill love.

Rock Crystal. (Madagascar) The phantom crystal within is caused by impurities during quartz crystal formation. These crystals may be used in meditation or journey work to track the ancestral stream.

Rutilated Quartz. (Brazil) With both needle-like rutile inclusions and a phantom crystal within, the energy of the quartz is magnified for increased healing benefits.

Smoky Quartz.

This stone was once popular for crystal gazing. Its high radium content may be helpful to people undergoing chemotherapy as it absorbs and neutralizes harmful influences. Use it also to heighten your connection with the earth and increase understanding of Nature and the environment.

Tourmaline. (Minas Gerais, Brazil) This example is an elbaite deposit on quartz. Tourmaline can absorb tremendous amounts of negativity, making the wearer sensitive to the needs of the body-earth. Combined in a setting with rose quartz, tourmaline rekindles the spark for lovers or close friends.

© Mark E. Gibson/Visuals Unlimited

© Ken Lucas/Visuals Unlimited

Wulfenite. This stone has a high lead content, aiding in meditation for healing purposes. It stimulates circulation and carries light energy through the body-earth.

Topaz. (Minas Gerais, Brazil) This crystal was once considered useful for ailments of the eyes—the stone was soaked in wine and rubbed on the eyes. Topaz is considered a sun stone, useful in strengthening the immune system. Blue topaz invites introspection.

© A. J. Copley/Visuals Unlimited

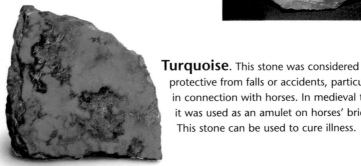

© A. J. Copley/Visuals Unlimited

Turquoise. This stone was considered protective from falls or accidents, particularly in connection with horses. In medieval times it was used as an amulet on horses' bridles. This stone can be used to cure illness.

Planet/Sign: Mercury/Virgo (exact cell salt equivalent); Jupiter/ Sagittarius

Stone Lore: This is an uncommon mineral. It occurs in several places in North America, such as Colorado, Arizona, Idaho, and California.

Medicine Uses: Jarosite brings dark or incomprehensible thoughts and ideas into sharp focus. Use this stone when contemplating both the shadow and light sides of your personality.

JASPER (see CHALCEDONY)*

KUNZITE (see SPODUMENE)

LAZURITE (LAPIS LAZULI)*

Crystal System: Isometric (Lazurite is part of the Sodalite group of minerals, though softer, lighter, and more finely grained)

Cell Salt: Silicate of sodium calcium and aluminum, with some sulphur (when lazurite also contains large amounts of calcite, diopside, and pyrite, it is called Lapis Lazuli)

Color: Azure-blue, violet-blue, and greenish blue

Energy: Magnetic

Element: Water

Planet/Sign: Moon/Cancer; Mercury/Gemini; Saturn-Uranus/ Aquarius

Stone Lore: Most of the world's lapis is currently found in Central Asia or Afghanistan.

Lapis lazuli was widely used as an ornamental stone in Greece and Rome, and was an important magical stone in ancient Babylonia, Assyria, and Egypt. Carved into bird and animal forms and made into jewelry, lapis was intended to protect the wearer from harm. Lapis was also fashioned into the shape of a heart, the Egyptian symbol for the "seat of life," as they believed that the stone could bring about resurrection following death. *The Egyptian Book of the Dead* shows a powerful lapis amulet in the form of an eye, most likely a ward against evil.

Medicine Uses: Lapis lazuli may be used to cure depression, sadness, mourning, and grief, as this stone exerts a strong influence in matters of the heart, including faithfulness and love. It may be used to treat physical heart conditions as well.

Lapis can keep the eyes healthy and the vision clear. Prepare an eyewash by placing lapis in a bowl of purified water overnight along with several drops of the herb eyebright. In the morning, splash the treated water into your eyes.

Lapis increases the psychic senses, as it works to fine-tune the feelings and instincts. Deep azure-blue, pyrite-streaked stones are potent healing medicine when worn with purposeful intent, and may help the wearer to develop clairsentient and telepathic powers.

Vedic healers suggest that lapis be set into a gold necklace for optimum benefits.

MALACHITE*

Crystal System: Monoclinic

Cell Salt: Basic copper carbonate

Color: Emerald green, grass green, and dark green

Energy: Magnetic

Element: Earth and Water

Planet/Sign: Venus-Neptune/Pisces

Stone Lore: Malachite was considered an appropriate talisman for children. Evil spirits were kept at bay and babies slept soundly if a malachite were attached to the side of the infant's cradle. Germans believed that the malachite would protect them against falling; it was thought to warn the wearer of impending disaster by cracking into several pieces prior to the incident. Because of the swirling patterns inherent in the stone, malachite was also popular in Italy as protection against the Evil Eye.

Ancient Egyptians carved malachite with an image of the sun, the source of light, as a protective amulet against necromancers, witches, and demons.

Malachite may be a psi-tech antidote to toxic plutonium wastes.

Medicine Uses: Malachite may induce feelings of sympathy and compassion for others. If worn consistently, it will restore vitality and life to a melancholy disposition.

We benefit from the soothing sensations of maternal warmth and love emanating through malachite crystal; however, malachite has a tendency to absorb negativity when used for healing purposes. Therefore, it must be thoroughly cleared and recharged after each use, or else it will fade and eventually begin to crack from retaining poisons and disease. The earth clearing method outlined in chapter 7 is best suited for malachite, as this stone regains strength and re-establishes equilibrium in the moist, fertile loam of Mother Earth.

MARCASITE*

Crystal System: Orthorhombic

Cell Salt: Disulfide of iron

Color: Pale brass-yellow to almost white metallic glitter

Energy: Magnetic

Element: Earth and Fire

Planet/Sign: Venus-Neptune/Taurus; Sun/Leo; Mars-Pluto/Scorpio

Stone Lore: Marcasite is mined in Missouri. This stone may also be collected in Oklahoma and Kansas, and in Mexico.

Marcasite disintegrates into a white powder, no longer resembling the original mineral, when left in its natural state.

Medicine Uses: Although marcasite crystals are in the process of dissolution, the existing polished specimens retain strong Earth energy and the power to calm the mind and instill emotional stability. Wear marcasite set in silver jewelry for optimum benefits.

META-ANKOLEITE

Crystal System: Tetragonal

Cell Salt: Potassium phosphate

Color: Yellow

Energy: Electric

Element: Fire

Planet/Sign: Mars-Pluto/Aries (exact cell salt equivalent); Saturn/Capricorn

Stone Lore: None available

Medicine Uses: Meta-ankoleite is difficult to obtain. However, should you get your hands on it, its healing energy resonates predominantly within the body-earth, as it purifies the blood and strengthens the central nervous system through the cellular groups in the head, heart, and sacral areas.

METEORITE (see MOLDAVITE)

MILKY QUARTZ (see QUARTZ)

MOLDAVITE

Crystal System: Hexagonal

Cell Salt: Moldavite falls into a subgroup of stones called tektites, which are silica based, or glassy meteorites

Color: Translucent olive green

Energy: Electric

Element: Air and Fire

Planet/Sign: Mercury/Virgo; Jupiter/Sagittarius

Stone Lore: Moldavite is a rare type of meteorite formed over fifteen million years ago. It is literally "fire from the sky." Meteorites have long been considered sacred by indigenous peoples all over the world because they carry the energies of the gods and spirit of the upper world to the middle world of Earth. Please refer to chapter 1 in the section called "Fire from the Sky" for further information.

Medicine Uses: Moldavite allows us to reach the deeper levels of conscious awareness, although I have found it to be a more effective medicine for those who have practiced some serious form of self-discipline, such as martial arts or spiritual pathwork.

The Otherworld quality of moldavite mesmerizes and quiets the senses. Use it to increase your knowledge of the relationship between heaven and Earth.

This stone works well with crystal, sugilite, aquamarine, diamond, lapis lazuli, opal, and peridot.

MOONSTONE*

Crystal System: Monoclinic

Cell Salt: Potassium aluminum silicate, sometimes with large amounts of sodium

Color: Transparent; opalescent; moonlike, silvery white light

Energy: Magnetic

Element: Water

Planet/Sign: Moon; Venus-Neptune/Pisces

Stone Lore: Moonstone is found in India and Australia.

The Orientals believed moonstone to be a "good luck" stone. It is also a sacred stone of India and is usually displayed on a yellow cloth in that country because yellow is considered a most holy color there.

In medieval times, Moonstone was a popular gift for lovers.

Medicine Uses: Due to the moving spirit-light inside the stone, moonstone is a trance-inducing gem and may be used for hypnotherapy, scrying, and all manner of divinatory work.

As in earlier times, the moonstone may be used to instill tender passion in the hearts of lovers. Place moonstone in your mouth during a full moon to read what the future holds for your love relationship.

Certain moonstones can be used to mark the waxing and waning of the moon. Observe your moonstone for one month's time by following the moving light within the stone. The light should appear as a small point on top of the stone during the new moon, as a round dot in the center during the full moon, and as a small point at the bottom of the stone during the last quarter moon.

Moonstone set in a silver ring should be worn on the right ring finger of a person who frequently suffers from emotional upsets during the new or full moon.

MORGANITE (see BERYL)

NEPHRITE (see JADEITE)*

NEWBERYITE

Crystal System: Orthorhombic

Cell Salt: Magnesium phosphate

Color: Gray, brown, or colorless

Energy: Electric

Element: Fire

Planet/Sign: Sun/Leo (exact cell salt equivalent); Venus-Neptune/ Taurus; Mars-Pluto/Scorpio

Stone Lore: None available

Medicine Uses: Newberyite dissolves old habit patterns and encourages the development of new and constructive thoughts, images, and actions.

Use this stone to strengthen the heart muscle, improve the circulation, and to relieve pressure on the spine resulting from a back injury.

OBSIDIAN*

Crystal System: Obsidian is an amorphous solid of glass substance formed from volcanic lava

Cell Salt: Spherulites of feldspar fibers with crystalline silica

Color: Generally black with smoky, translucent to transparent edges; also black mixed with gray, reddish brown, mahogany, dark green, forming thin bands or marbled

Energy: Magnetic

Element: Earth and Fire

Planet/Sign: Saturn; Mars-Pluto

Stone Lore: Obsidian can be found all over the world.

The Aztecs made images of the god Tezcatlipoca or "Smoking Mirror" of obsidian. Obsidian mirrors were used for divination in Mexico and other South American countries. The English magus, Dr. John Dee, used Mexican obsidian as a scrying stone.

Some Native American tribes fashioned arrowheads, knives, and spear points from obsidian crystal.

Medicine Uses: Round spheres of obsidian are still sold in Mexico today; use them in place of clear quartz crystal for divinatory purposes.

Obsidian can aid the decision-making process. It is capable of both attracting and repelling negativity, and must therefore be used with care. This stone is excellent for grounding and all situations wherein you are forced to undergo drastic changes beyond your control.

APACHE TEARS* are a natural, rough, circular, or cylindrical form of obsidian. These dense black crystals may be carried in a medicine pouch or set in silver jewelry as a powerful protective amulet against all negative influences.

OLIVINE (see PERIDOT)

ONYX (see CHALCEDONY)*

OPAL*

Crystal System: Opal is an amorphous stone, and not linked with any specific system.

Cell Salt: Hydrous silica, often with some iron and aluminum

Color: White (White Opal); Yellow, red, pink (Fire Opal); brown, green, gray, or blue flames in a black field (Black Opal); pale blue, green, orange (Precious Opal); colorless

Energy: Neutral-electric

Element: Air

Planet/Sign: All

Stone Lore: Objects have been known to fossilize in opal, such as the skeleton of a small serpent that became opalized by natural processes found in Australia in the early 1900s. Obviously, this "serpent" opal is a very powerful amulet in the eyes of mystics, shamans, healers and occultists.

In the Middle Ages, the opal was called the eye-stone, as it was thought to be formed from the eyes of children.

Due to misinterpretation of the novel *Anne of Geierstein* by Sir Walter Scott, the opal is thought to be unlucky. In fact, many people are still extremely superstitious regarding this stone and will not wear it under any circumstances. However, the stone is relatively neutral, and simply magnifies the hidden strengths or weaknesses of the wearer.

Medicine Uses: The opal has been gravely misunderstood. It is difficult to wear because it is very fragile and needs special care and conscious attention. If you wear an opal ring, for example, be careful not to bang your hand against a hard surface, or the stone may break.

The key to understanding opal is balance. Like the malachite, opal will crack if you are out of sync, in danger, or under stress.

For this reason, wear opal to ensure your safety, to protect your position against those who wish you harm, or simply to bring good fortune.

Opal may be used to cure eye diseases as well as to render the wearer invisible.

The natural, youthful luster of hair may be maintained by wearing opal barrettes or earrings that touch the hair in some way. If the stone begins to fade, you may need to increase your vitamin intake or change your shampoo to keep your hair looking shiny and healthy.

Wear opal on the right index finger in a gold ring, or set it in a gold necklace.

BLACK OPAL is an exceptionally lucky stone. However, it may also bring us to the brink of the abyss where dwells the shadow-self who must be faced if we are to realize who we are and why we are here.

FIRE OPAL contains the energies of all the heavenly bodies. Use it to balance the seven spirit energy centers, or to assist you in astral projection or shamanic journey work.

PRECIOUS OPAL* flames with the gentle spirit of love. This form of opal may be used in all healing work. It is an especially valuable stone for the healer as a diagnostic tool, for the colors of the stone will fade out when it is swept over a troublesome auric or body area.

WHITE OPAL is a powerful supersensory receiver of lunar energies. It is also an excellent medicinal stone for the treatment of skin inflammations such as boils, pimples, and rashes, and for general elimination of toxins from the body.

PEARL (see SEA SHELL)*

PERIDOT

Crystal System: Orthorhombic

Cell Salt: Magnesium iron silicate

Color: Yellow-green; dark yellow-green (Olivine)

Energy: Electric

Element: Earth and Fire

Planet/Sign: Venus/Taurus; Sun/Leo; Mars-Pluto/Scorpio

Stone Lore: Peridot is mined in the United States, Brazil, Russia, and Egypt.

In Biblical times the peridot was considered to be a great spiritual teacher capable of producing miracles, while in medieval times a peridot engraved with the image of a mule was used to predict the future.

Peridot and olivine crystals have been found in meteoric stones.

Medicine Uses: Peridot is both a receiver and transmitter of healing energy. It is a helpful assistant in clearing emotional and physical congestion.

There is a connection between peridot and the digestive, assimilative, and eliminatory systems, and it may be used to bring light into the dark, hidden regions of the bowel.

While peridot is strong and resistant, it has been known to sustain damage if the central nervous system is unduly stressed or permeated with atmospheric, auric, or physical toxins. Many years ago, the peridot set into my quartz crystal pendulum became chipped at a time when I was under extreme duress. The stone had absorbed all the bad vibes that were sent in my direction. I worked to clear the energy from the stone and could not use it for a long time thereafter. One day, several years later, I once again picked up the pendulum. Upon close inspection, the chip was no longer visible. The stone had healed and once again enjoys gainful employment as a divinatory tool and protective amulet.

OLIVINE is a darker close relative of peridot crystal. The same medicine uses apply to olivine.

PETRIFIED WOOD*

Crystal System: None

Cell Salt: Fossilized plant matter with varied mineralization

Color: Shades of brown, with stripes of black or gray

Energy: Magnetic

Element: Earth

Planet/Sign: Saturn; Taurus/Virgo/Capricorn

Stone Lore: Petrified wood comes from trees and is found worldwide. It is very old and is a record-keeper for the Earth.

Medicine Uses: As trees have similar circulatory systems to our own, petrified wood may be used for skin inflammations, muscle diseases, and circulatory problems.

Astral travel and journey work may be facilitated by placing a piece of petrified wood at the small of the back.

Petrified wood is deeply connected to the Earth and the environment, and can make us more aware of our environment.

PIPESTONE (Catlinite)

Crystal System: Isometric

Cell Salt: Hydrous aluminum silicate

Color: Brick red

Energy: Magnetic

Element: Earth, Air, and Fire

Planet/Sign: Mercury/Gemini; Moon/Cancer; Saturn-Uranus/ Aquarius

Stone Lore: The traditional Native American pipe bowl is made of catlinite from Pipestone Quarry in Minnesota. The stem may be made of stone or wood. The pipe is perhaps the most sacred object in Native American spirituality. It was first given to the Lakota Indians by White Buffalo Calf Woman, and is now used by many Indian tribes for prayer. It is not merely a symbol of that which is sacred—the pipe itself is sacred. Unci Kunshi, the Grandmother Earth, lives in the bowl. The stem represents Tunkashila, the Grandfather Sky. Sometimes the pipe is decorated with beads, feathers, and painted symbols.

Medicine Uses: Pipestone is used primarily to fashion the sacred pipe, which is always handled with the utmost respect. The bowl is filled with *canshasha*, the red willow bark tobacco, or herbs such as sage or wild cherry bark. Then the pipe is lit and the smoke offered to Grandfather Sky, Grandmother Earth, and to the four directions. As the pipe is shared among the People, the smokers become one with the earth and sky, because they are filled with the Great Mystery of visible breath.

If you wear pipestone beads or keep a piece of natural pipestone in your medicine pouch, recognize that it is a great blessing to have this stone in your possession. Always treat pipestone with the utmost respect and remember to include the Lakota and all indigenous people in your thanksgiving.

POTTERY SHERDS

Crystal System: Isometric

Cell Salt: Hydrous aluminum silicate

Color: Creamy white; reddish brown; black; often with hand-painted surfaces

Energy: Magnetic

Element: Earth

Planet/Sign: Mercury/Gemini; Moon/Cancer; Saturn-Uranus/Aquarius

Stone Lore: Pottery sherds have been found in archeological sites all over the world. Some sherds are thousands of years old, while others are relatively new, perhaps constructed in the last hundred years or so. In the United States, many sites (such as American Indian burial grounds) have been plundered, but in the southwestern portion of the country much pottery remains in its natural state, perhaps because the dry desert air and soil acts as a preservative.

Many rock hounds collect pottery sherds, especially those belonging to Native American peoples. I have come across folks selling sherds at flea markets and crafts fairs. I've also seen sherds on the desert floor, ripe for the taking.

No doubt pottery sherds are beautiful, exotic, and charged with vital force. I believe they contain the living essence of the indigenous culture by and through which they were formed. Some individuals want to be a part of the American Indian culture, and perhaps capturing the sherds is the only way they know how. However, while it is all right to admire pottery sherds, I cannot stress enough how wrong it is to sell them or to own them for whatever reason. All pottery sherds belong to the descendants of the culture that produced them. In the case of American Indians, this means that the descendants are likely to be living people.

Anyway, politeness and politics aside, there may be bad "juju" attached to pottery sherds. As rangers at national parks such as Chaco Canyon and Bandelier National Monument in New Mexico can attest, many unhappy tourists have mailed their finds back to the park following a run of bad luck which they connected to the pottery sherds.

PYRITE*

Crystal System: Isometric

Cell Salt: Iron disulfide, often with substantial amounts of nickel and cobalt

Color: Pale to brass-yellow, sometimes tarnished with a brownish film of iron oxide

Energy: Electric

Element: Air

Planet/Sign: Mercury/Gemini; Moon/Cancer; Saturn-Uranus/ Aquarius

Stone Lore: Pyrite is found in North America, Chile, and Peru.

It is used for divination and healing by the medicine people of some North American Indian tribes.

Mexican Indians make beautiful pyrite mirrors, which like the Mexican obsidian mirrors, were perhaps also used for scrying.

Pyrite is also known as Fool's Gold because it has often been mistaken for real gold due to its yellow coloring.

Medicine Uses: Polished pyrite is an excellent divinatory tool. It may also be used to focus the attention, transmit healing energy, or to attract money and good health.

PYROPE (see GARNET)

QUARTZ*

Crystal System: Hexagonal

Cell Salt: Silicon dioxide

Color: Colorless and transparent (Rock Crystal); clear with rutile inclusions (Rutilated); clear with black inclusions (Tourmalinated Quartz); purple (Amethyst); pink, rose-red (Rose Quartz); clear yellow (Citrine); pale brown to black (Smoky Quartz); milk-white (Milky Quartz); glistening green with mica or hematite inclusions (Aventurine); opalescent with asbestos inclusions (Cat's Eye); lustrous yellow to brown (Tiger's Eye)

Energy: Electric

Element: Fire and air

Planet/Sign: Sagittarius (exact cell salt equivalent); Mercury/Virgo

Stone Lore: The most beautiful rock crystal quartz comes from Arkansas.

Quartz crystals have been used for magical and/or healing purposes since the beginning of time as we know it. Some say the crystal was known in the days when Atlantis and Lemuria were still on the map. I have heard that Pleiadeans and other alien nations use clear quartz crystal to power their space ships, but I couldn't verify it personally.

Magicians and occultists have used crystal balls for scrying and divination for centuries, while crystal bowls have long been popular tools for aura balancing and healing. Water-filled crystal bowls were once used to dowse the auric and physical bodies for imbalances.

Modern technology would be hard pressed without the clear quartz crystal as it is used in the simplest radio transmitters and receivers as well as in state-of-the-art computers, to store, release, and regulate electromagnetic energy.

New Age psi-tech specialists run several steps ahead of science, having developed many extraordinary crystal tools, such as quartz crystal rods and staffs, crystal headgear, time communication generators, force fields and energy shields, force knives, and autoelectromags.

Quartz Crystal comes in several different structures and forms:

Clusters are highly evolved crystals that emit strong healing vibrations; they may be used to clear the atmosphere, to cleanse other stones, or as proximity stones for altars, desk tops, window sills, or night tables. Clusters appear as several crystals joined together at the base or flat end of the crystal.

Generator or single-point crystals channel and ground energy.

Double-terminated points both transmit and receive energy, and may be used to dissolve energy blockages in the body-earth. A double-terminated crystal has a point on each end.

Tabular crystals are flat in appearance and may serve as a bridge or connecting link between polar opposites.

Record keepers hold ancient knowledge and the deepest secrets of creation; if a crystal is a record keeper, it will have a small triangle on one of its six faces.

Teacher crystals contain vast resources of personal and cosmic knowledge. They can be found in any shape, size, or variety of quartz. A teacher crystal is like the "stone of light" mentioned in chapter 7: it appears into your life out of nowhere, and you'll know it when it comes to you.

Rainbow crystals contain the full color spectrum of the rainbow inside. These crystals are sacred, as they unite and integrate heaven and Earth.

Phantom crystals contain small, pyramid-shaped inclusions that mark the growth pattern of the stone; these crystals may be used in meditation or journey work to track the ancestral stream.

Medicine Uses: Many spiritual practitioners, from traditional shamans to contemporary healers, have the versatile quartz crystal in their possession. Indeed, the remedial uses pertaining to this stone are many. It can be taken internally when formulated into an elixir (see chapter 5, Crystal Medicine 5: Sun and Moon Water Tonic for Wholeness of Being), worn as jewelry, carried in a medicine pouch, or combined with metals and other stones to be fashioned into various transformational tools.

AMETHYST* has an extensive history and is a marvelous healing crystal. The Egyptians made amethyst amulets in the form of animals as early as 2000 B.C. The Hebrews believed that this stone could induce dreams and visions, while the Greeks thought it could prevent drunkenness.

Amethyst has the power to control all types of harmful behavior, sharpen the mind, increase the memory, and strengthen the immune system. It is able to calm an overly passionate nature. This stone may also protect soldiers from harm, and help hunters find food in the wild.

All physical, emotional, and mental problems may be treated with amethyst. The deep purple variety is an excellent stone for hospice and hospital workers, as amethyst helps to alleviate the emotional sense of attachment to the body-earth for those about to cross over into the Otherworld.

AVENTURINE is a Nature stone. It brings peace, tranquility, and serenity when used as a touchstone, and may be used to attract abundance and prosperity when worn on the body or carried in a medicine pouch.

CAT'S EYE QUARTZ is not quite as distinct as the chrysoberyl Cat's Eye; however, the stone may be used to the same effect.

CITRINE* was a prized stone among Celtic and Scottish peoples. It is energizing, invigorating, and positive. It increases motivation and relieves feelings of inertia, thereby improving digestion and clearing congestion from the internal organs. Citrine may work to purify the blood as well.

Citrine may be used as a blessing stone to offer love and gratitude to the Great Spirit, as well as to open the heart center. It magnifies thoughts and emotions, and can assist in manifesting desires.

There is a special correspondence between citrine and the element of air. It is therefore extremely beneficial in clearing negative atmospheres. Use citrine as a touchstone to instill warmth and love following treatment of panic disorders, anxiety attacks, fears, phobias, and obsessions.

Avoid purchasing stones that have been heat processed; obtain only deep yellow crystals without any traces of purple coloring.

HERKIMER DIAMOND comes from Herkimer, New York. This stone is a very old storehouse of ecological memory. It acts as a filter to release toxins from the body-earth as well as boosting the immune system. Use it to increase the energy and healing qualities of other stones.

MILKY QUARTZ is not a very popular stone, probably due to its dense, white color. However, it symbolizes the here and now, and may help those following a spiritual path to recognize life as an eternal process. If you work with a milky quartz long enough, the stone will eventually become rock crystal clear, and so will you.

ROCK CRYSTAL,* also known as clear or white crystal, is the most popular form of quartz. Shamans have used rock crystal for hundreds of years because it grants them the power to rise to the sky, or fly to the top of the World Tree.

This stone amplifies whatever influences are present in a particular person, place, or thing. It is a dedicated healer, and may be used to remove physical, emotional, mental, and spiritual blockages. It directs energy into sluggish auric and body areas to accelerate the healing process. Rock crystal can be worn or used by anyone for any purpose imaginable, or used in conjunction with all other crystals, gems, and minerals to treat specific problems. It will magnify the effects of individual stones and adjust the healing medicine to suit individual energy needs.

Sometimes the high vibrational frequencies and strong electromagnetic currents of energy emitted through rock crystal may increase emotional sensitivity and overactivate the central nervous system of highly receptive individuals. If you start to feel "burned out" from overexposure, remove it from contact with the body, wrap it in silk or deer hide, and place it on your night table until your body adjusts to the increased energy levels engendered by the stone.

ROSE QUARTZ* imparts a gentle, soothing influence, and is especially beneficial for calming the emotions. It is quite restorative when healing old traumatic memories and wounds stemming from childhood abuse, abandonment, neglect, separation, or divorce.

Rose quartz makes an excellent gift for lovers, children, and anyone in need of sympathy and affection. Choose pale, translucent shades of pink radiating with rainbow infractions for this purpose.

RUTILATED QUARTZ* contains needlelike rutile inclusions (see RUTILE). The energy of rutile is magnified by the quartz for increased healing benefits. See Rutile for further information.

SMOKY QUARTZ* is a stone of the lower world of soul. This stone was once popular among crystal gazers. It can be used when praying to heal ancestors, and may be carried by people undergoing chemotherapy and radiation therapy due to the high radium content in the stone. Usually, however, it is best to avoid the heavily irradiated crystals, not because they are dangerous, but because the internal integrity of the stone is affected as a result of this form of microwave heat-processing.

Natural smoky quartz crystals absorb and neutralize harmful influences and shield the wearer from harm. This stone may also heighten our connection with the Earth as well as increase our understanding of Nature and the environment.

TIGER'S EYE QUARTZ* contains the gentle grounding energy of Earth. It is stabilizing, enduring, and can help build confidence and increase one's sense of security. Tiger's Eye can help us to recognize our personal resources and use our abilities to attain our dreams because it is an excellent stone for developing and encouraging discipline and concentration, especially in children. This stone may bring abundance, prosperity, and financial independence to the wearer.

Polished and set in copper, tiger's eye is a powerful charm against harmful spirit intrusions. The brown, red, and blue tiger's eye crystals are equally effective in their healing potencies.

TOURMALINATED QUARTZ* contains black tourmaline inclusions. The essence of black tourmaline is magnified by this special stone (see **TOURMALINE**).

REALGAR

Crystal System: Monoclinic

Cell Salt: Arsenic sulfide

Color: Deep red to orange color (may become yellow upon exposure to light)

Energy: Electromagnetic

Element: Fire and Water

Planet/Sign: Mars-Pluto; Venus-Neptune/Pisces

Stone Lore: Realgar is mined in Utah, Nevada, and California.

Medicine Uses: Realgar is an enigmatic mineral because it is simultaneously crude and gentle. It can benefit those who wish to neutralize and refine their sexual energy.

RHODOCHROSITE*

Crystal System: Hexagonal

Cell Salt: Manganese carbonate with some calcium, iron, magnesium, and zinc

Color: Pink, rose-red, dark red, or brown

Energy: Electric

Element: Fire

Planet/Sign: Mercury-Uranus/Virgo; Jupiter/Sagittarius

Stone Lore: Rhodochrosite is a fairly new discovery in the mineral kingdom.

Medicine Uses: Rhodochrosite may be used to treat conditions affecting the upper respiratory system. It is an excellent blood purifier and may be worn at heart level to stimulate the circulation, or set in a copper bracelet.

   Place rhodochrosite crystal under your pillow at night to enhance and help you remember your dreams.

   This stone is compatible with malachite.

RHODONITE*

Crystal System: Triclinic

Cell Salt: Manganese silicate, often with some calcium

Color: Brownish red, flesh-red, and pink

Energy: Electric

Element: Earth and Fire

Planet/Sign: Venus/Libra

Stone Lore: Rhodonite is found in the United States, Brazil, India, Japan, and Russia.

Medicine Uses: This stone may engender balance through strength of will. As a "karma" stone, it may also accelerate the inevitable consequences of cause and effect.

Pink rhodonite helps us to monitor our thoughts, desires, words, actions, and responses, while the brownish red and flesh red stones encourage self-discipline, stability, moral courage, and faith.

ROCK CRYSTAL (see QUARTZ)*

ROSE QUARTZ (see QUARTZ)*

RUBELLITE (see TOURMALINE)

RUBY (see CORUNDUM)*

RUTILATED QUARTZ (see QUARTZ)*

RUTILE

Crystal System: Tetragonal

Cell Salt: Titanium dioxide, often with substantial amounts of iron

Color: Red, reddish brown, black

Energy: Electric

Element: Fire and earth

Planet/Sign: Mars-Pluto/Aries; Saturn/Capricorn

Stone Lore: Rutile may be found worldwide in igneous and meta-morphic rock formations. It occurs in quartz, orthoclase, and barite crystalline structures.

Medicine Uses: Rutile both disciplines and structures our approach to life. It filters out painful memories and may be used when investigating the shadow side of the self.

SAPPHIRE (see CORUNDUM)*

SEA SHELLS*

Crystal System: None

Cell Salt: Calcium phosphate with silica and other minerals which comprise the homes and skeletons of sea creatures

Color: Gray to white with opalescent pink, orange, yellow, white, blue and green (Abalone); red, pink, white, gray or black (Coral); white to yellow (Cowrie); opalescent white, cream, blue, gray to black (Pearl); red to orange with whitish pink striations (Spiny Oyster); brown to black, brownishgreen, brownish yellow (Tortoise)

Energy: Magnetic

Element: Water

Planet/Sign: Moon; Cancer/Scorpio/Pisces

Stone Lore: Sea shells are found wherever there is an ocean. They have been used since the Stone Age for practical, decorative, and magical purposes.

Medicine Uses: Sea shells symbolize boundless growth, the emotions, hearing, and the ear canals. Any shell may be carried to treat calcium deficiencies, mood disorders, and bone diseases such as osteoporosis.

Sea shells work well when combined with crystals, feathers, or other shamanic tools. They are especially useful to counterbalance overly dynamic energies due to their watery nature.

ABALONE,* also known as Ear Shell, is found in warm tropical waters off the coasts of California, South America, Japan, and China. This shell is commonly used for decorative purposes in jewelry. Some American Indians use the shell to hold spirit offerings such as tobacco and blue corn. It also makes a great holder for burning sage, sweetgrass, and cedar. Abalone may be helpful to build and protect the heart muscle as well as aid the digestion.

CORAL is found in oceans all over the world. Almost all cultures use coral for reasons pertaining to magic, religion, or health. The ancients believed that those who carried red or white coral could control the weather. Coral was thought to stop hemorrhaging and endow the wearer with wisdom.

The Pueblo Indian people of the Southwestern United States make beautiful animal fetishes of red coral. Hindu healers use red coral as a blood purifier, claiming it can calm anger, jealousy, and hatred when worn on the ring or index finger of the right hand. Black coral is popular in the Caribbean for talismans and amulets to absorb negativity and protect the wearer from harm. Pink coral is soothing, healing, and pleasure-giving, while white coral may be used to synchronize and stabilize the rhythms of the body-earth.

These lighter shades of coral may grow pale when worn against the skin, warning the wearer of illness, weakened vitality, or toxicity.

In general, coral is good for the bones and central nervous system, especially the brain stem. Because it quiets the emotions, it may be beneficial in the treatment of certain mental/emotional illnesses.

When mixed with diamond, ruby, emerald, and pearl, and suspended at the entrance of a house, coral makes a powerful amulet that will protect from harm all who dwell inside.

Peri-menopausal women may wear red coral to time ovulation and other cycles associated with the menses, and to help regulate the hormones. The coral fades when there is hormonal imbalance and brightens again when the hormones return to normal.

Coral should always be used in its whole and natural state for magical purposes.

COWRIE SHELL* is most commonly used for decorative purposes, such as on ceremonial garments and jewelry. It may also be used as a spirit offering or in sympathetic magic wherein the energy of the sea is required.

PEARL* is a round, calcified object produced in the bodies of oysters or other fresh or saltwater shellfish as a result of sand or some other foreign material irritating the creature's sensitive skin.

Pearls may be worn to purify the blood and to regulate body rhythms. For this reason, they are especially beneficial for pregnant or menopausal women. However, pearls tend to absorb emotional energy, so please clear the stone before wearing it again if it has accompanied you into a negatively charged situation. Otherwise, pearl is a soothing influence, and can help you to overcome difficult obstacles.

A pearl water tonic can be made to increase vitality, relieve eye strain, and soothe burning urination: place several small pearls in water overnight and drink the following day. This tonic is a natural antacid and anti-inflammatory.

Pearl should be set in silver and worn on the right ring finger.

SPINY OYSTER contains the same medicine properties as red and pink coral; however, it is not as potent.

TORTOISE SHELL is where the tortoise or turtle lives when he's feeling reclusive. Of course, hiding out didn't keep him from losing his shell! Personally, while I admit to having tortoise shell in my collection, I hate the idea of systematically harvesting this gentle creature. Should you acquire a tortoise shell, be sure it is not from an endangered species.

Tortoise shell is strong medicine. It increases fertility and brings good luck and abundance into your life. It also serves to remind us of the ecology, as we all live on Turtle Island—the body of Mother Earth. For maximum benefits, stuff the tortoise shell with herbs such as sage, cedar, and sweetgrass and place it on your altar, or fit a deerskin pouch into the shell, fill it with a quartz crystal, corn kernels, and mountain tobacco, and carry it on your person.

SERPENTINE

Crystal System: Monoclinic

Cell Salt: Basic magnesium silicates (Antigorite and Chrysolite)

Color: Olive green, black to yellow-green, brown, yellow, and white (rare); often with white streaks or striations

Energy: Magnetic

Element: Earth and Water

Planet/Sign: Venus-Neptune/Pisces

Stone Lore: Serpentine is found in North America, England, and Italy.

Medicine Uses: Italian streghe or witches believe that small pebbles of serpentine afford protection from the bites of venomous creatures, mainly because the green color streaked with white resembles snakeskin. If a person has already been bitten by a snake or poisonous insect, the stone is thought to draw out the toxins. These benefits may be had only if the stone is in its natural state and has never come into contact with iron.

Serpentine is also an excellent tool for psychic development, as it cleanses and conditions the emotions.

SMITHSONITE*

Crystal System: Hexagonal

Cell Salt: Zinc carbonate, often with some iron

Color: White, gray, colorless, green, blue, yellow, purple, pink, or brown

Energy: Electric

Element: Air and Fire

Planet/Sign: Mercury/Virgo; Jupiter/Sagittarius

Stone Lore: Smithsonite is named for James Smithson, the founder of the Smithsonian Institution. It is found in the United States, Australia, Greece, and Italy.

Green and blue smithsonite crystals will eventually evolve similar spirit qualities as chrysocholla and turquoise.

Medicine Uses: Smithsonite helps us bring empowerment to action by enhancing our ability to complete desired goals. Also, use this stone to clarify the mind, instill a sense of security, and ease difficulties in relationships.

SMOKY QUARTZ (see QUARTZ)*

SODALITE*

Crystal System: Isometric

Cell Salt: Sodium aluminum silicate with chlorine

Color: Blue, gray, white, colorless or green, often streaked with white

Energy: Electromagnetic

Element: Air and Water

Planet/Sign: Moon/Cancer; Mercury/Gemini; Saturn-Uranus/ Aquarius

Stone Lore: This stone is found in North America, Brazil, and France.

Medicine Uses: Sodalite may be useful for balancing the metabolism. It is also a good shock absorber, and may be used to combat the negative effects of radioactive materials and treatments, such as X-rays, radiation, and chemotherapy.

Sodalite is a record-keeper, and is easily impressed with new ideas and emotions. It is an excellent memory bank and can help you follow the track of previous incarnational experiences. Due to the sensitivity of the stone, new and previously unused crystals are best for personal use.

SPESSARTINE (see GARNET)

SPINY OYSTER (see SEA SHELL)

SPODUMENE

Crystal System: Monoclinic

Cell Salt: Lithium aluminum silicate

Color: White, gray, yellowish; emerald green (Hiddenite); pink to purple (Kunzite)

Energy: Magnetic

Element: Water

Planet/Sign: Venus-Neptune/Pisces

Stone Lore: Spodumene comes from North Carolina.

Medicine Uses: This stone suggests ideas associated with fertility, beauty, growth, depth, and love.

HIDDENITE represents harmony through struggle and conflict. It has a definite affinity for Nature and the plant world. This stone teaches us to revere all our relations, and to recognize our place in the scheme of all created things.

KUNZITE has the interesting ability to absorb sunlight or artificial light and then give it off in the dark. Use it to relieve stress as well as to elicit feelings of love, compassion, and good will toward others.

Due to its high lithium content, kunzite crystal may also be used to balance certain biochemical disorders, such as schizophrenia and manic depression.

STERCORITE

Crystal System: Triclinic

Cell Salt: Sodium phosphate

Color: White, colorless, yellow and brown masses or nodules

Energy: Electric

Element: Air

Planet/Sign: Venus-Neptune/Libra (exact cell salt equivalent)

Stone Lore: None available

Medicine Uses: Stercorite increases knowledge and understanding through logic and reason. Use it when you need to make an important, unbiased decision, as stercorite allows for practical, objective, rational thinking, uncolored by primal fear or emotions.

SUGILITE

Crystal System: Hexagonal

Cell Salt: Potassium sodium ferric lithium silicate

Color: Pale lavender to deep magenta or purplish black; sometimes streaked with green or white

Energy: Magnetic

Element: Water and earth

Planet/Sign: Mercury/Virgo; Jupiter/Sagittarius

Stone Lore: Sugilite is a relatively new stone. It has gained increasing popularity for use in Native American and New Age jewelry.

Medicine Uses: Sugilite is a powerful healing stone. The deep magenta stones may be used to heal painful emotions arising from repressed moodiness, hurt, resentment, and anger. Streaked with green, sugilite further soothes the untamed aspects of the instinctual nature, engendering forgiveness and protection. There is some indication that sugilite can help ease the discomfort of migraine headaches when placed on the third eye or at the base of the skull. Polished sugilite points are excellent transformational tools for releasing old habit patterns.

As sugilite evolves, it will prove to be a most effective medicine in the alternative treatment of cancer as well as AIDS and other sexually transmitted diseases (STDs).

Sugilite is highly compatible with turquoise, red coral, onyx, chrysoprase, and abalone.

SYLVANITE

Crystal System: Monoclinic

Cell Salt: Telluride of gold and silver; metallic

Color: Silver-white to steel gray

Energy: Magnetic

Element: Water

Planet/Sign: Venus-Neptune/Pisces

Stone Lore: This mineral was originally found in Transylvania, so perhaps it could be used to ward off vampires, or to attract them. It is also mined in small quantities in Ontario, Canada, as well as in California and Colorado.

Medicine Uses: Sylvanite has tremendous conductive and transmissive capabilities because it contains both gold and silver. It engenders feelings of social conscience as well as heartfelt love and affection for humankind.

Hold sylvanite in your receptive hand. Imagine that you are a tree. Your head is the top, your heart is the trunk, and your feet are the roots, rooted in Mother Earth. Feel love well up in your heart. Send this love energy above, to Sky Father, and below, to Earth Mother. Feel love returning to you from above and below, meeting in the middle, in your heart.

SYLVINE

Crystal System: Isometric

Cell Salt: Potassium chloride

Color: Yellow, blue or red

Energy: Electric

Element: Air

Planet/Sign: Gemini (exact cell salt equivalent); Jupiter/Cancer; Saturn-Uranus/Aquarius

Stone Lore: None available

Medicine Uses: The cubic shapes formed by sylvine represent stability, establishment, balance, and permanence. This stone may be used when you are feeling nervous, upset, or insecure.

THERNADITE

Crystal System: Orthorhombic

Cell Salt: Sodium sulphate

Color: White to brownish white or gray

Energy: Magnetic and electric

Element: Earth, Fire, and Water

Planet/Sign: Venus/Taurus (exact cell salt equivalent); Sun/Leo; Mars-Pluto/Scorpio

Stone Lore: This mineral occurs in many places around the world, such as Spain and North America.

Medicine Uses: Thernadite crystal may be used to awaken and balance the throat, heart, and belly centers. It is helpful for calming emotional upsets, soothing sore throats, and abating heart palpitations due to anxiety.

Rub thernadite crystal in a circular motion on the carotid artery located on the right and left sides of the neck for several minutes to quell a panic or anxiety attack.

TIGER'S EYE (see QUARTZ)*

TOPAZ*

Crystal System: Orthorhombic

Cell Salt: Aluminum fluorsilicate

Color: Colorless, pale yellow-green, yellow to orange yellow, dark orange to red-orange; blue

Energy: Electric

Element: Air and Fire

Planet/Sign: Venus/Taurus; Mercury/Gemini; Jupiter/Sagittarius

Stone Lore: Topaz is mined in the United States, Brazil, and Sri Lanka.

Topaz was recommended by St. Hildegarde of Bingen as a cure for loss of vision; the stone was soaked in wine and then rubbed on the eyes, and the wine presumably drunk when treatment was complete. During the fifteenth century it was used as a cure for the plague.

Medicine Uses: Topaz has long been considered a sun stone, and may be used to increase vitality, strengthen the immune system, and generally bring about good health. Set in gold, topaz will protect the wearer from harm.

If you happen to channel spirit entities, yellow topaz is the stone for you. Clear blue topaz crystal enhances introspection. The colorless varieties of the stone bring wisdom and illumination. Green and yellow stones foster innocence and creative imagination, while orange and red topaz may empower the wearer with courage and conviction.

Topaz should be worn in a gold necklace or on the right index finger in a gold ring.

TORTOISE SHELL (see SEA SHELL)

TOURMALINATED QUARTZ*
(see QUARTZ or TOURMALINE)*

TOURMALINE*

Crystal System: Hexagonal

Cell Salt: Complex silicate of boron and aluminum; varied composition of inherent substances

Color: Pink and green (Elbaite and Watermelon Tourmaline); blue (Indicolite); red to purple-red (Rubellite); dark orange-brown (Dravite); black; clear; cat's eye with inclusions

Energy: Electromagnetic

Element: Air, Earth, and Fire

Planet/Sign: Mercury/Virgo; Jupiter/Sagittarius

Stone Lore: Tourmaline is mined in the United States, Brazil, Australia, Mexico, and Russia. It became a known gemstone in the eighteenth century.

When heated, tourmaline will develop opposing electrical charges at the opposite ends of the crystal, indicating extreme focusing power.

Medicine Uses: Tourmaline works to purify the entire body, including the auric field. It is a wonderful stress reducer, perhaps due to the sheer beauty of the stone. Worn against the skin at heart level, tourmaline conveys peace and tranquility, and helps to organize scattered thoughts and emotions.

This stone is also well known for its ability to absorb tremendous amounts of negativity, both from the wearer and from the environment, and it can make the wearer more sensitive to the immediate needs of the body-earth.

Black tourmaline repels rather than absorbs negative energy. This stone is valuable during crises and situations causing emotional duress. It may be used to combat life-threatening diseases as well as to fight pyschic attack, spirit possession, and harmful spirit intrusions.

Cat's eye tourmaline should only be used by those who are very attracted to it, as it seems to block energy rather than encourage it.

Clear tourmaline is sort of like a low-key quartz. It works to cleanse and detoxify the immune system, and may be useful in the treatment of eye problems and biochemical nerve disorders such as epilepsy.

DRAVITE contains the essence of the sun and earth. It is very helpful when worn while cultivating the garden.

ELBAITE* crystallizes in both green and pink stones. The green crystals soothe an overly dynamic temperament, stimulate creativity and rejuvenate the body-earth. The pink stones enhance affection in difficult relationships, and will help you to accept and love yourself. Pink or green elbaite tourmaline combined with rose quartz and set in silver is an excellent gift for lovers, life-mates, or close friends who need to rekindle love in their relationship.

INDICOLITE sublimates and heals discord, chaos, conflict, doubt, and confusion.

RUBELLITE stimulates the will, the instincts, and the memory. It can put us in touch with past life experiences, thus enabling us to better understand our motivations in this lifetime. It works to heal disturbing emotional influences that rise to the surface with no apparent cause. Large rubellite crystal formations may be kept in well-trafficked areas of homes where physical, verbal, or mental abuse is a common occurrence.

WATERMELON TOURMALINE will work to heal any situation where extreme conflict is a factor, as the combined pink and green coloration shows us how opposites work together in harmony to achieve beautiful results. Use this stone to anticipate which direction a particular situation is going to take, so that you may act accordingly.

Watermelon tourmaline has a strong affinity for green and growing things, and is useful for inspiring a deep, abiding reverence for the natural beauty of Earth.

TURQUOISE*

Crystal System: Triclinic

Cell Salt: Hydrous basic phosphate of copper and aluminum, with some iron

Color: Sky blue, blue-green, apple-green, pale green; streak white

Energy: Magnetic

Element: Earth and Air

Planet/Sign: Venus-Neptune/Libra

Stone Lore: Turquoise is found primarily in the United States, France, and Tibet. The name "turquoise" was originally the French word for Turkish.

In the thirteenth century, turquoise was the stone to wear if you didn't want to fall off a horse, a building, or a precipice, or have a house or wall fall on your head. This latter applied especially if the turquoise was set in gold. Thirteenth-century Turks often attached turquoise to the bridles of their horses as amulets to keep them from becoming ill as a result of overexertion. In medieval times, turquoise was considered to be the quintessential "horse-amulet."

During the seventeenth century, the turquoise was considered to be a man's stone; women rarely wore it.

Turquoise was also thought to be an accurate timepiece. If the stone were suspended from a thread held between the thumb and forefinger (like a pendulum), the vibrations would cause it to strike the side of a glass in such a way as to tell the correct time.

Back in the 1800s, much turquoise was mined at Mount Chalchiuihtl in the Cerrillos Hills in New Mexico. The Pueblo Indians of this region greatly disapproved of this action, because to them the turquoise was (and still is) a sacred stone. In fact, a medicine man would not receive proper recognition without a turquoise in his possession. A mining disaster in the Cerrillos Hills back then buried many of the Indian miners alive, and the area remains haunted to this day.

Turquoise is still a most popular stone for use in southwest American Indian jewelry, and is worn for decorative and ceremonial purposes.

Medicine Uses: Native Americans from New Mexico and Arizona carve turquoise into animal shapes such as frogs, birds, squirrels, bears, coyotes, and even porpoises and whales. The fetishes are usually strung together on a necklace and worn as a protective amulet. Turquoise is also a strong talisman for the hunter: a turquoise tied to a gun would ensure a swift and accurate kill.

Turquoise is a very dependable health barometer. This stone tends to draw toxins from the body and is likely to fade or darken if you are harboring disease in your system. I have seen this many times, and sometimes the effects are quite dramatic.

A friend of mine suffered from chronic skin inflammations due to an early, life-threatening illness. Whenever a portion of her skin was about to abscess, her turquoise ring, which was normally colored light blue-green, would turn to a dark forest green. When the condition was cleared up, the ring would return to its original shade.

This stone can also be used to cure illness: the Shoshone Indians use turquoise and jade together under water, and send prayers to heal a sick mind or body.

Hindu mystics say turquoise brings wealth if you look at it on the first day after the new moon. The Navajos have a similar idea (previously mentioned in chapter 7) involving turquoise and a coyote, a trickster with decidedly lunar tendencies.

Turquoise may be offered in friendship, as the spirit in the stone is quite amicable about transferring allegiance from one person to another.

In general, turquoise is wonderful for healing, protection, and self-definition. This stone really lets you know who you are.

UVAROVITE (see GARNET)

VIVIANITE

Crystal System: Monoclinic

Cell Salt: Hydrous phosphate of iron

Color: Blue, green, or colorless when freshly excavated, but darkens when exposed to light

Energy: Magnetic

Element: Water

Planet/Sign: Venus-Neptune/Pisces (exact cell salt equivalent)

Stone Lore: Vivianite is found in New Jersey, Maryland, Colorado, Idaho, and Quebec, Canada.

Medicine Uses: Vivianite regulates the delicate endocrine system. It aids us in defending the body-earth against disease by instilling in us a positive mental outlook on life. This stone may be useful for treating severe depression and as a preventative medicine when the body is threatened by illness as a result of long-term, negative mental/emotional states of consciousness.

WATERMELON TOURMALINE (see TOURMALINE)

WULFENITE*

Crystal System: Triclinic

Cell Salt: Lead molybdate

Color: Yellow, orange, brown, and yellowish gray

Energy: Electric

Element: Air

Planet/Sign: Venus-Neptune/Libra

Stone Lore: The choice mining places for wulfenite crystal occur in the American Southwest and Mexico.

Medicine Uses: Wulfenite stimulates the circulation and carries light-energy throughout the body-earth. Owing to its high lead content, wulfenite may be used during meditation to focus healing energy on specific bodily areas.

ZIRCON

Crystal System: Tetragonal

Cell Salt: Zirconium silicate, often with some hafnium

Color: Gray, brown, and green; transparent red (Hyacinth); and colorless or smoky (Jargoon)

Energy: Electromagnetic

Element: Fire and Earth

Planet/Sign: Mars/Aries; Saturn/Capricorn

Stone Lore: Zircon is found in North America, France, and Italy.

Medicine Uses: This stone helps us to synthesize our actions so that we are focused to accomplish our goals.

HYACINTH or **JACINTH** has an esoteric connection to the lion, and may be used for courage, vitality, and strength of will. It is a traveler's amulet, and can keep you from getting sick when worn on an extended journey. It may also help you in obtaining favors on plane flights or in hotels.

Hyacinth can help dissolve high cholesterol and may also help in the treatment of angina if set in gold and worn on the Sun (third) finger of the receptive hand (see page 77). Treat panic disorders and anxiety attacks by combining hyacinth with jargoon set in silver and worn at heart level.

Hyacinth can induce sleep if placed under the pillow between the waning and waxing moon, perhaps because it relieves nightmares and protects against bewitchment.

JARGOON absorbs negativity and brings order to chaotic situations. This stone may be used as a tool for unearthing secrets, finding lost treasures, and looking into shadows, especially our own.

And May the Quartz be with You...
Sherry Black and Everett Buss' garden sentinel.

EPILOGUE

THE DWARF

Little man in cavern deep,
Ancient one, 'neath earth so creep
Stealthily, dark wisdom borne
Age-old long before first dawn
Coveted, bound secrecy,
Dwarf tongue held most silently.

Further, darkened bowels tread,
Downward fine carved rock so led;
Toiled treasure, buried hoard,
Favored jewels, the heart's adored,
Cool the miner's burning soul,
Turn to diamond, eyes of coal.

Gem-wrought fate shown to wonder,
Ever sealed, spell drawn under,
Stood 'midst goblets silver-starred
Defended when the dragons warred;
Lust drunk, bearded half-man caught
'Mid the wisdom ever sought.

Sandra Reading Kadisak, Mountain Legends

Sculptured Clay Image of One of the Little People

CRYSTAL RESOURCE GUIDE

Crystal Medicine

Marguerite Elsbeth (*Senihele*, Sparrow Hawk)
P.O. Box 1535
Pena Blanca, NM 87041
505–465–0806

(European and Native American folk-healing, Medicine bags, Astrology, Tarot)

Robert "Dude" Perry
P.O. Box 5537
Chubbeck, ID 83202–0004

(Shoshone-Navajo medicine work)

The Little People: Mountain Legends
6535 Tahawash
Cochiti Lake, NM 87083
505–465–0217

(One of a kind, signed and numbered, sculptured clay images of "The Little People;" see image on page 208.)

Crystal, Rock, and Mineral Specimens/ Photographs/Artwork/Jewelry

Everett Buss/Sherry Black
P.O. Box 221
Crestone, CO 81131
719–256–4280

(Stone people sculpture and special stones for sale; crystal imagery points for beauty and meditation)

Joel Glick
1700 El Camino Real, Rue 9–15
San Francisco, CA 94080

(Dramatic, museum-quality crystal jewelry)

Sound and Color

"Chakra Chips"
Oceana Lowry
P.O. Box 7870
Albuquerque, NM 87194
505–243–3232

(Copper-bound, stained-glass squares, triangles and circles in the colors of the chakra points)

Metal Elixirs

Oxygen for Life, Inc.
11555 Rancho Bernardo Road
San Diego, CA 92127–1441
619–673–6363/FAX 800–673–4883

(Colloidal gold and silver)

The Ayurvedic Institute
P.O. Box 23445
Albuquerque, NM 87192–1445

(Information and/or treatment with metal elixirs)

Crystal Mines and Other Areas of Interest:

The Crater of Diamonds State Park, near Murfreesboro, Arkansas, is great for amateur prospectors, who are allowed to keep whatever stones they find. Most of the diamond specimens found here are small, though it's possible to get lucky. (Free)

Ka-da-ho, located on an old channel of the Missouri River near Murfreesboro, Arkansas, was the home of mound-building Indians about a thousand years ago. Nearby, a small museum displays stones, shell, and pottery artifacts. (Free)

Several rock shops display specimens of novaculite and quartz crystal at **Mount Ida**, a resort town located at the western end of Lake Ouachita. There are crystal mines near the city where you may hunt for interesting pieces. (Fee)

Arkansas diamond, an unusual brown rock shot with quartz crystals, can be purchased at the rock shop at the roadside location known as **Blue Springs**, south of Jessieville, Arkansas. Keep going for ten miles and you will come to a mountain of quartz and to Coleman's Mine, where visitors may hunt for crystals. (Fee)

Sulphur Hot Springs, located in Pagosa Springs, Colorado, provides room, board, and natural sulphur baths in a beautiful setting. (Fee)

Visit **Rock Hound State Park** in Deming, New Mexico, open all year round. Here you can camp out under the stars and gather agate, quartz, and other stones that live on the land for free, up to fifteen pounds of rocks per person. (Fee)

Canyonlands National Park—Squaw Flats-Needles District/Hwy 191, approximately thirty miles south of Moab, Utah, is where the rock kingdom lives. Here you will find a campsite, drinking water, Anazasi ruins, and rock and more rock. (Fee)

Green Beach, situated in Maui, Hawaii, is comprised of tiny olivine (peridot) crystals, the ultimate healing stone for physical difficulties of any kind.

The **Tucson Gem and Mineral Show** takes place every February in Tucson, Arizona. Make reservations six months in advance for this one. Call the Tucson Chamber of Commerce for information, dates, and special events.

The **largest gem and mineral show in the world** occurs in Quartzite, Arizona throughout the month of February. Miners and a Native American powwow are the focal points of the show. Pack up the RV or bring camping gear for this one. Call the Quartzite Chamber of Commerce for information, dates, and special events.

The **Deming, New Mexico, rock and mineral show** happens in the fall. Call the Deming Chamber of Commerce for details.

Lunar Phases

Llewellyn's Magical Almanac or *Llewellyn's Moon Sign Book*
P.O. Box 64383
St. Paul, MN 55164–0383
1–800–THE–MOON
(To track the phases of the moon)

GLOSSARY

Alchemy: Working with Nature to bring about earthly perfection, while at the same time working toward self-transformation and integral wholeness.

Aliens: Beings from outer space.

Asteroid: Any of the small planets or planetoids between the orbits of the known planets of our solar system.

Astrology: Literally, the science or doctrine of the stars, once related to astronomy.

Astronomy: The current and accepted mode of treatment by science of the heavenly bodies.

Atom: A tiny particle that combines with elements of other particles like itself to produce a compound substance.

Atomic structure: The concept of an atom as an electrically charged center that magnetically charged electrons revolve around in various orbits.

Autoelectromag: A subatomic particle power pistol.

Combustion: Oxidation generating both heat and light, thus instigating the sudden inflammatory conditions necessary to produce change.

Contraction: Inertia or energy drawn inward.

Crystal System: Crystals always grow in accordance with simple, mathematical laws. The six crystal systems delineate the symmetry of crystals, gems, and minerals. Crystallographers, those who have made a scientific study of the form, structure, properties, and classifications of crystals, can fit any crystal into one of the six basic crystal systems.

Constellation: A group of fixed stars that lie along the ecliptic or zodiac, based on the point of the Vernal Equinox where the ecliptic intersects the celestial equator. There are twelve generally known constellations in what is called the Zodiac of Constellations, including Aries, Taurus, Gemini, Cancer, Leo, Virgo, Libra, Scorpio, Sagittarius, Capricorn, Aquarius, and Pisces.

Cubic system (see Isometric)

Dipyramid: A duplicate form in which the crystal faces intersecting the vertical and equilateral axes create two points, one at the top and one at the bottom.

Dodecahedron: A crystal with twelve plane faces.

Electricity: A current of energy generated by heat and light, consisting of positive (electric) and negative (magnetic) charges which attract each other.

Electromagnetism: Electromagnetism is the product of an indefinable energy that underlies the physical forces of electricity (positive or dynamic energy), magnetism (negative or passive energy), light, and heat. In this context, electromagnetic energy was known as spiritual ether to the alchemists, *ain soph aur* or "the limitless light" to Qabalists, *prana* or *prakriti* to the Hindus, and "Great Spirit" or "Great Mystery" to the Native Americans. Here I refer to it as "spirit energy," based on the theory that electromagnetism can be generated by the spirit, mind, and emotions as well as by physical means.

Electron: Any of the negatively charged particles that form a part of all atoms.

Expansion: Momentum or an outward flow of motion.

Extraterrestrial: Otherwordly or celestial, not pertaining to the earth.

Galactic human: In astronomy, galactic refers to the Milky Way or Galaxy.

Gravity: This is a term used in physics to indicate the force that pulls all bodies in the earth's sphere toward its center.

Hexagonal (or Trigonal): Crystals generally occurring in prismatic or columnar formations, with rounded triangular or hexagonal cross sections. Characteristic hexagonal forms are three or six-sided prisms, pyramids, and rhombohedrons. The similar trigonal system is often included within the hexagonal system.

Hydrogen: An inflammable, odorless, colorless gas, the lightest of all known substances.

Isometric: Generally blocky or ball-like crystal forms, having many similar, symmetrical faces. These stones characteristically form as cubes, octahedrons, and dodecahedrons, either single or in various combinations. The isometric crystal system is also known as the cubic crystal system.

Light: Everything is made from or is reciprocal with the electromagnetic frequencies, of which visible light is a part. Every substance in the universe is connected to light in its essential composition. Light disperses throughout the cosmos and pervades all of space.

Magnetism: The power to attract, such as occurs in the gravity of earth, emotional affinity, or personal charm and allure.

Meteor: An object rapidly entering the earth's atmosphere from outer space, white-hot and visible as a result of friction with the air. Also, a shooting star, or any atmospheric phenomena, such as a rainbow, hail, or lightning.

Meteorite: A solid mass comprised of metallic or mineral substances that has fallen to the earth from outer space.

Momentum (see Expansion).

Monoclinic: Generally stubby crystalline forms, with tilted matching faces at opposite ends, suggesting a distorted rectangle. These crystals characteristically form as prisms and pinacoids.

Neutrino: A neutral particle with very little mass or charge and having little or no direct interaction with matter.

Nuclear fission: The splitting of atoms that converts mass into energy.

Octahedrons: A crystal with eight planed surfaces.

Orthorhombic: Generally short and stubby crystalline forms with a diamond-shaped or rectangular cross section. They characteristically form as four-sided prisms, pyramids, and pinacoids (open forms comprised of two parallel faces).

Photons: The parts of electromagnetic energy that move, such as the energy inherent in light, X-rays, gamma rays, and cosmic rays.

Pinacoid: A plane to which two crystal axes are parallel.

Planets: In astronomy, any heavenly body with apparent motion, or that shines as a result of sunlight and revolves around the sun. In astrology, any heavenly body that directs a person's life and influences the personality, as well as accentuates the living properties within the mineral, plant, and animal kingdoms.

Pleiades: According to Greek myth, Atlas and Pleione had seven daughters, who were placed among the stars by Zeus. Thus, in astronomy the Pleiades comprise a large group of stars in the constellation of Taurus, six of which are visible and represent the daughters of Atlas. The seventh daughter is "lost," as she is invisible to the naked eye.

Pleiadians: Beings from the Pleiades and/or people who claim to be from the Pleiades.

Preservation: That which maintains balance when meeting with the pull of gravity, and exists at the heart of all life-forms—terrestrial or extraterrestrial.

Proton: The fundamental particle in the nuclei of all atoms, carrying a positive electrical charge.

Psi-tech: First there was high-tech and now there is psi-tech, a technique dealing with energy particles, waves, and fields, and used for tapping into and directing the powers of imagination.

Pyramid: A crystal form in which the faces intersect the vertical and lateral axes.

Quantum physics: The natural science of energy.

Science: The systemized knowledge of nature and the physical world.

Solar system: The sun and planets that revolve in orbits around the Sun in response to the Earth's gravitational pull.

Star: Any heavenly body seen as a fixed point of light in the night sky. The Sun is a also star.

Striation: One of a series of fine parallel lines on the face of a crystal; also, a groove or channel in a rock surface.

Strong force: The energy that binds the nucleus of atoms together.

Supernova: A star that suddenly increases in brilliance and then gradually grows fainter.

Tetragonal: Long, slender, or sometimes needlelike crystals, which characteristically form into four-sided prisms, pyramids, and dipyramids.

Thermonuclear energy: The heat energy released in nuclear fission, which causes atoms to break apart.

Triclinic: Flat crystals with sharp edges and sharp, thin cross sections. No right angles occur on faces or edges. All triclinic crystal forms are pinacoids.

Trigonal (see Hexagonal).

UFO: An unidentified object usually perceived as flying at varying heights and speeds and sometimes regarded as light phenomena, hallucinations, secret military aircraft, or a vehicle from another planet.

Weak force: The energy responsible for certain kinds of radioactivity.

SELECTED
BIBLIOGRAPHY

Ahlquist, Cynthia, ed. *Llewellyn's 1996 Magical Almanac*. St. Paul: Llewellyn Publications, 1995.

Andrews, Ted. *Crystal Balls & Crystal Bowls: Tools for Ancient Scrying & Modern Seership*. St. Paul: Llewellyn Publications, 1995.

Bowman, Catherine. *Crystal Awareness*. St. Paul: Llewellyn Publications, 1994.

Budge, E. A. W. *The Book of the Dead*. London: Longman & Co., 1895.

Bulfinch, Thomas. *Bulfinch's Mythology*. New York: Avenel, 1978

Calverley, Roger Anthony. *The Healing Gems*. Ontario: Bhakti Press, 1983.

Chocron, Daya Sarai. *Healing with Crystals and Gemstones*. York Beach, ME: Samuel Weiser, Inc., 1986.

Cirlot, J. E. *A Dictionary of Symbols*. New York: Philosophical Library, 1983.

Crow Dog, Leonard, and Richard Erdoes. *Crow Dog: Four Generations of Sioux Medicine Men*. New York: HarperCollins Publishers, Inc., 1995.

Cunningham, Scott. *Cunningham's Encyclopedia of Crystal, Gem & Metal Magic*. St. Paul: Llewellyn Publications, 1988.

de Santillana, Giorgio, and Hertha von Dechend. *Hamet's Mill: An Essay on Myth and the Frame of Time.* Boston: Gambit Inc., 1969.

Eliade, Mircea. *The Forge and the Crucible: The Origins and Structures of Alchemy.* New York and Evanston: Harper Torchbooks, 1971.

_____. *Shamanism: Archaic Techniques of Ecstacy.* Princeton: Princeton University Press, 1972.

Frazer, F.R.S., F.B.A., Sir James George. *The Golden Bough: A Study in Magic and Religion.* New York: The Macmillan Company, 1923.

Fuller, John Grant. *The Interrupted Journey.* Alexandria, VA: Time Life, Inc., 1993.

Glick, Joel, and Julia Lorusso. *Healing Stoned: The Therapeutic Use of Gems & Minerals.* Albuquerque, NM: Brotherhood of Life, 1985.

Gray, F.R.S., Henry. *Gray's Anatomy.* New York: Bounty Books, 1977.

Holden, Alan, and Singer, Phylis. *Crystals and Crystal Growing.* New York: Anchor Books, 1960.

Hudson, Charles. *The Southeastern Indians.* The University of Tennessee Press, 1976.

Huson, Paul. *The Devil's Picture Book.* London: Sphere Books Ltd., 1972.

Jung, C. G. *The Collected Works of C. G. Jung, Volume 13, Alchemical Studies.* Princeton: Princeton University Press, 1976.

Kunz, George Frederick. *The Curious Lore of Precious Stones.* New York: Dover Publications, Inc., 1971.

Lad, Dr. Vasant. *Ayurveda: The Science of Self Healing, A Practical Guide.* New Mexico: Lotus Press, 1984.

Lewis, Thomas H., *The Medicine Men: Oglala Sious Ceremony and Healing.* Lincoln, NE: University of Nebraska Press, 1990.

Lonegren, Sig. *Spiritual Dowsing.* Somerset: Gothic Image Publications, 1986.

Means, Russel, with Marvin J. Wolf. *Where White Men Fear to Tread: The Autobiography of Russel Means.* New York: St. Martin's Press, 1995.

Ranade, Subhash. *Natural Healing through Ayurveda*. Salt Lake City: Passage Press, 1993.

Raphaell, Katrina. *Crystal Enlightenment: The Transforming Properties of Crystals and Healing Stones*, Vol. I. New York: Aurora Press, 1985.

Reader's Digest. *America From the Road: A Motorist's Guide to Our Country's Natural Wonders and Most Interesting Places*. New York/Montreal: The Reader's Digest Association, Inc., 1982.

Sibley, Uma. *The Complete Crystal Guidebook: A Practical Path to Self-development and Healing Using Quartz Crystals*. New York: Bantam Books, 1987.

Smith, Michael G. *Crystal Power*. St. Paul: Llewellyn Publications, 1994.

Smith, Michael G., and Lin Westhorp. *Crystal Vision: Shamanic Tools for Change and Awakening*. St. Paul: Llewellyn Publications, 1994.

_____. *Crystal Warrior: Shamanic Transformation & Projection of Universal Energy*. St. Paul: Llewellyn Publications, 1992.

The Audubon Society. *The Audubon Society Field Guide to North American Rocks and Minerals*. New York: Knopf, 1978.

Stevens, Jose, Ph.D. and Lena Stevens. *Secrets of Shamanism: Tapping the Spirit Power Within You*. New York: Avon Books, 1988.

Storm, Hyemeyohsts. *Seven Arrows*. New York: Ballantine Books, 1972.

Strieber, Whitley. *Communion*. New York: Beech Tree Books, 1987.

Talbot, Michael. *The Holographic Universe*. New York: Harper Perennial, 1992.

Three Initiates. *The Kybalion: Hermetic Philosophy*. Chicago: Yogi Publication Society, 1940.

Young, Jacqueline. *Acupressure for Health: A Complete Self-Care Manual*. San Francisco: Thorsons, 1994.

Ywahoo, Dhyani. *Voices of Our Ancestors: Cherokee Teachings from the Wisdom Fire*. Boston: Shambhala Publications, 1987.

INDEX

INDEX

☽ REACH FOR THE MOON

Llewellyn publishes hundreds of books on your favorite subjects! To get these exciting books, including the ones on the following pages, check your local bookstore or order them directly from Llewellyn.

ORDER BY PHONE
- Call toll-free within the U.S. and Canada, 1-800-THE MOON
- In Minnesota, call (651) 291-1970
- We accept VISA, MasterCard, and American Express

ORDER BY MAIL
- Send the full price of your order (MN residents add 7% sales tax) in U.S. funds, plus postage & handling to:

  Llewellyn Worldwide
  P.O. Box 64383, Dept. K258-5
  St. Paul, MN 55164–0383, U.S.A.

POSTAGE & HANDLING
(For the U.S., Canada, and Mexico)
- $4.00 for orders $15.00 and under
- $5.00 for orders over $15.00
- No charge for orders over $100.00

We ship UPS in the continental United States. We ship standard mail to P.O. boxes. Orders shipped to Alaska, Hawaii, The Virgin Islands, and Puerto Rico are sent first-class mail. Orders shipped to Canada and Mexico are sent surface mail.

International orders: Airmail—add freight equal to price of each book to the total price of order, plus $5.00 for each non-book item (audio tapes, etc.).

Surface mail—Add $1.00 per item.

Allow 2 weeks for delivery on all orders.
Postage and handling rates subject to change.

DISCOUNTS
We offer a 20% discount to group leaders or agents. You must order a minimum of 5 copies of the same book to get our special quantity price.

FREE CATALOG

Get a free copy of our color catalog, *New Worlds of Mind and Spirit*. Subscribe for just $10.00 in the United States and Canada ($30.00 overseas, airmail). Many bookstores carry *New Worlds*—ask for it!

Visit our website at www.llewellyn.com for more information.

Animal-Speak
The Spiritual & Magical Powers of Creatures Great & Small

Ted Andrews

The animal world has much to teach us. Some are experts at survival and adaptation, some never get cancer, some embody strength and courage while others exude playfulness. Animals remind us of the potential we can unfold, but before we can learn from them, we must first be able to speak with them.

In this book, myth and fact are combined in a manner that will teach you how to speak and understand the language of the animals in your life. Animal-Speak helps you meet and work with animals as totems and spirits—by learning the language of their behaviors within the physical world. It provides techniques for reading signs and omens in nature so you can open to higher perceptions and even prophecy. It reveals the hidden, mythical and realistic roles of 45 animals, 60 birds, 8 insects, and 6 reptiles.

Animals will become a part of you, revealing to you the majesty and divine in all life. They will restore your childlike wonder of the world and strengthen your belief in magic, dreams and possibilities.

0–87542–028–1
400 pp., 7 x 10, illus., photos, softcover $19.95